WHAT PEOPLE ARE SAYING ABOUT *CLEAR THE STAGE* . . .

"*Clear the Stage* isn't just another how-to book for pastors. It has plenty of practical suggestions to apply in leadership and worship. What deeply inspired me is how Scott Wilson and John Bates pointed me to the Lord, reminded me of His power and glory, and encouraged me to 'let God be God' in our worship services. This is a must-read for pastors and leaders."

Reverend Wilfredo "Choco" De Jesús, senior pastor of New Life Covenant Church, Chicago, IL, and author of *Amazing Faith* and *In the Gap*

"Quite often, pastors are looking for 'the next big thing' to implement in their churches. In *Clear the Stage,* Scott Wilson and John Bates look backward and forward. They point us back to the beauty and power of our traditions, and they show us the necessity of trusting the Spirit's leading in worship today."

Mark Batterson, *New York* [illegible] r of *The Circle Maker*

"What I like about *Clear t* [illegible] the both/and model rather than the either/or church in which I was raised. I remain unashamedly Pentecostal and agree wholeheartedly with the message of this book—how to have a healthy biblically based Spirit-led and Spirit-filled church. Many of these experiences will parallel yours and many will be unique—but they will all be encouraging and enhancing."

Dr. Sam Chand, author of *Leadership Pain: The Classroom for Growth,* www.samchand.com

"With passion, clarity, conviction, and unwavering truth, Scott Wilson and John Bates point us back to Spirit-led services that produce Spirit-led lives and to a cause worth giving our lives to. *Clear the Stage* will enlighten you to truths that unleash a world-changing adventure with God and His church."

Obed Martinez, senior pastor, Destiny Church, founder of PassionatePastors.com

"I know firsthand how essential it is to be open to the work of the Spirit of God in ministry. If you're a pastor or leader looking to let go of the heavy burden of playing the central role in planning and orchestrating worship experiences, *Clear the Stage* is for you. This timely new book by Scott and John is full of biblical insight to restore Spirit-empowered distinctives to modern worship—encouraging all those involved in ministry to let go and let God move in the hearts of His people."

Rob Hoskins, president of OneHope

"*Clear the Stage* is not for pastors and leaders who are content with the status quo, it's for those who carry the burden to see God move in our 'everyday' through the power and presence of the Holy Spirit. This book is quantifiably practical yet truly inspiring. It sets a new bar for all leaders as we face the fact that to be truly successful we must make space for God in every facet of our lives. I highly recommend this terrific, easy to read book to those who are interested in kingdom work and are busy about the mandate presented by Habakkuk 'to see the knowledge of the Lord cover the earth as the waters cover the seas.'"

Ossie Mills, executive director of Empowered21

"Today's trend of highly creative and well-produced services can often work against moments of spontaneous and sovereign moves of the Spirit. If there's anything our churches need today, it's the manifest power of God moving supernaturally in our services. Scott and John speak honestly about the journey of stripping away anything and everything that could potentially distract from the main thing. *Clear the Stage* will challenge you to yield to the whispers of the Spirit and enjoy the freedom that comes from keeping Jesus at the center of it all."

Scotty Gibbons, national youth ministries strategist for the Assemblies of God/My Healthy Church

"When an author writes from the perspective of personal encounter, the pages of the book not only hold valuable information but, more importantly, serve as a compass for all who walk the same path. The message within the pages of *Clear the Stage* has dramatically moved me, and I pray for a generation of believers to take the unchanging character of God, the inspired Scriptures, and the fluidity of encounter based in culture and run with it. Scott and John model the sacrifice some will make and the hunger all should have to see the presence of the Spirit impact multitudes in very practical ways."

Heath Adamson, senior director of youth ministry for the Assemblies of God/My Healthy Church and author of *The Bush Always Burns*.

"*Clear the Stage* is outstanding! It's a must-read! In this day of increasing complexity, simplicity is required. Acts 3:19 declares there are times of refreshing in the Spirit. These moments require humility for church leaders: Are you willing to let God be right? They require flexibility: Are you willing to adjust? And they require agility: Are you willing to walk in new ways? Scott and John address these issues clearly."

Gerald Brooks DD, Grace Outreach Center; author of *Understanding Your Pain Threshold*

"I am an eyewitness to the transformation of The Oaks Fellowship. Scott Wilson could have played it safe and stayed in control of his very effective Sunday morning. But he opened his heart and his church to the movement of the Holy Spirit and saw God show up in power. If you're hungry for renewal in your life or your church, this book will give you the courage to seek it out. All it takes is giving God a chance."

Earl Creps, PhD., DMin., pastor, church planter, author of *Off-Road Disciplines* and *Reverse Mentoring*

CLEAR THE STAGE

MAKING ROOM FOR GOD

SCOTT WILSON & JOHN BATES

Published by Influence Resources
1445 N. Boonville Ave.
Springfield, Missouri 65802
www.influenceresources.com

Cover design by PlainJoe Studios www.plainjoestudios.com
Interior formatting by Anne McLaughlin

ISBN: 978-1-68154-004-7
Printed in the United States of America

18 17 16 15 • 1 2 3 4

This book is dedicated to the courageous people of The Oaks Fellowship. I will forever be grateful for your support and encouragement. Thank you for living the pages of this book and letting God continue to write new chapters in our church. You could have run away when God began to turn our church upside down, but you didn't. Instead, you jumped in with both feet!

—Scott Wilson

This book is dedicated to those involved in the prayer ministry of Freedom Fellowship International. You have valiantly chosen to put the needs of others above your own. You not only understand freedom in Christ, you humbly model it for others. Your untiring, selfless prayers make the kingdom of God a better place. Thank you for being you!

—John Bates

CONTENTS

FOREWORD

Young leaders. I meet them every day from all around the globe. They are brilliant, technologically savvy, passionate in heart, and committed to absolute authenticity. These potential world-changers are longing for genuine expressions of the Christian faith devoid of pretense or self-promotion. They comprehend more and more that we must get self out of the way so the fullness of the Spirit can flow through us. They are trusting God to create thoroughly real, vibrant, and organic spiritual life in their churches, families, and lives . . . something naturally supernatural.

These leaders are as quick to share their struggles as they are to celebrate their victories. Rigorous honesty, they are convinced, is the foundation for a genuine experience of the Spirit's presence, purpose, and power. This kind of honesty takes them off the pedestal and makes them approachable. This new generation of emerging leaders usually doesn't view themselves as superstars, but as men and women whose primary role is to equip others to serve joyfully and effectively. As pastors Scott Wilson and John Bates point out, everyone gets a flame; everyone is sent by God to live, love, and serve. Scott and John understand and live by these vital kingdom principles.

Scott's church is one of the bright spots in an American Christian landscape that too often lives on props, entertainment, and the latest cultural trends. The refreshing move of the Holy Spirit in Scott's life and at The Oaks promises to have a profound impact on a new generation of leaders. My prayer is that what God is doing at The Oaks will spread across America and around the world. We desperately need authentic, transforming encounters with the Holy Spirit in the twenty-first century. This book leads us down both the new and ancient pathway of raw honesty and heartrending sincerity that explodes into God-moments where heaven touches earth and we are changed. These encounters at the altar of honesty will give us the courage to tear down every altar of hypocrisy we have built.

It's already happening. I know because I've seen it. We recently asked Scott to speak to our students at Oral Roberts University. He told the story of how God directed him to clear the stage of his heart and make room for God to move in his church. As Scott spoke, the Holy Spirit worked. After his message, hundreds came to the front to meet with him and our chaplains to ask for prayer. These students and future leaders connected with Scott's message of laying down anything that would hinder them from experiencing the fullness of the Spirit—even a good thing that has taken God's rightful place in the center of their affections. For our students and staff, it was a Spirit-led, Spirit-empowered encounter, one that will have an impact on them for the rest of their lives. I, too, was convicted to search my own heart for anything I have allowed to subtly crowd out Christ's presence. It was a great day for all us to *clear our stage.*

I'm equally grateful for John's life and ministry. Without his honesty, courage, and tenacious love for Scott, the things God is doing in and through Scott at The Oaks wouldn't be happening. All of us need someone like John to encourage us and challenge us. We may not always want to hear a prophetic word, but we desperately need someone to love us enough to speak truth to our hearts. Don't miss this story in their book. The strength of their relationship is one of the catalysts for God's powerful, tender, life-changing work.

These two leaders and their message are vitally important for the church today, in our country and around the world. Everywhere I travel and from all the letters and emails I receive, I see leaders who thirst for authentic, Spirit-filled expressions of their faith. The old wineskins won't hold the new wine. These leaders need a new vision, a new vocabulary, and a new relevance in their cultural contexts. They need *Clear the Stage*. The message of this book gives them hope and handles—hope that God will enable them to move in the gifts so that the supernatural power and love of God will transform lives, and clear, practical steps they can take as they trust God in this pursuit.

Local churches, communities, and people around the world are waiting for Christian leaders who are humble enough to clear away anything that hinders the full expression of the Spirit of God . . . and desperate enough to invite God to do what only God can do. I hope you will be one of these leaders.

—Dr. Billy M. Wilson, president of Oral Roberts University

SECTION 1

TURNING POINT

CHAPTER 1
A NEW DAY

The principles and practices in this book were born in a powerful and challenging relationship. The Scriptures tell us that God works most often and most powerfully through the "iron sharpening iron" of vulnerable, inspiring, and honest connections with other believers. We don't need a hundred of those relationships, but we desperately need a few. The book in your hands is the product of this kind of connection.

In this chapter, both of us will tell the story of how we met and how the relationship began to grow. Scott will be the voice in chapters 2 through 9, and John will be the voice in chapters 10 through 15. Then both of us will share our hopes in the last chapter.

FROM SCOTT . . .

John's question hit me right between the eyes.

He asked, "Scott, will you give God one minute?"

The year was 2012, and I was out to breakfast with my

good friend and fellow pastor John Bates. He had called earlier that morning with the urgent message: "Scott, we need to meet!"

Over the years, I had grown to trust John and his spiritual insights. He walks with God with a prophetic anointing. I had learned to listen when he speaks. That morning at breakfast, however, his question confused me. I instantly thought, *Of course I'll give God a minute. I've given Him my life, haven't I? Everything I have belongs to Him.* But I suspected that wasn't what John was asking. Somehow, his question seemed deeper . . . more significant . . . more threatening.

John took a deep breath and continued to push. He could tell by the look on my face that I really didn't understand his question. He reworded it: "Scott, would you give God one minute of your service on Sunday morning?"

I suddenly realized he was challenging my leadership, my style, and even more, my identity as the kind of pastor I had become. The timing, though, seemed very odd. I had just begun a new teaching series called "Open." It was, ironically, about hearing the voice of God. John's question was pushing me out of my well-insulated comfort zone.

Immediately, I thought of several quick and easy answers to his question, but I also realized none of them worked. Instead, many more questions popped into my mind:

- How much was I depending on my style of leading and teaching instead of trusting in the Spirit?

- Was I willing to trust God instead of my own carefully honed instincts as a pastor?
- Was I ready for "Open" to be an accurate description of the way our hearts responded to God?
- Was I willing for it to be an accurate description of *my own heart*? And finally,
- Was I ready to trust God to lead, shape, and empower the Sunday morning services at The Oaks?

I thought I was making real progress in processing the question, but John wouldn't let up. He drilled deeper: "Let me put it another way. Are you just saying 'Okay God, here's my plan for the service. Will You please bless it?'"

I knew better than that. I reacted with more than a hint of defensiveness: "No! That's not what I want at all!" I calmed down, took a deep breath and explained, "I want God's plan because I know it already comes with His blessing!"

His next question rocked me back on my heels. "But Scott, are you really living by that?"

"What do you mean?" I asked. Before he said another word, my thoughts swirled. Did John really think I was running the services at The Oaks without God . . . and thinking that's fine? I certainly didn't believe that was true. I prayed and prepared for hours each week. I studied and rehearsed to make sure I was fully ready for the services every Sunday. What else did God want from me?

Then, just like an Old Testament prophet, John went “all in” and put his cards on the table. “Scott, I’m telling you right now what I feel God is saying. He’s telling me that you’re going to Him with your plans and your ideas, and you’re saying, ‘Okay God, please let Your anointing be upon this. Be glorified in this service. Please work in people’s lives.’”

John shifted in his seat and looked me straight in the eye. “Scott, when was the last time you were quiet in the service and gave God a minute? When was the last time you actually gave God the opportunity to speak in one of your services?”

God was asking me to "clear the stage" for His Spirit to work in power and love in our services.

So that was it. We were down to the real question. I finally understood. God had sent my friend John to challenge me at the core of my soul. This wasn’t about a program, a style of worship, my teaching, or the order of service at our church. It was about my heart, my hopes, my faith, and my identity as a pastor. God was asking me to “clear the stage” for His Spirit to work in power and love in our services. He was asking me to relinquish control of Sunday morning—the hours that shaped my identity most powerfully and I protected most carefully—to the control of the Holy Spirit.

To be honest, I wasn't too surprised to hear a word from God through John. For years God had been using him to draw me deeper into what He wanted for my life and my ministry at The Oaks. In many ways, we had been building toward this moment since we first met.

Years before, when our church moved into its current location in Red Oak, Texas, John felt led to bring his entire congregation to the dedication service. John was convinced even then that God was calling our two congregations to walk together. During the service, the Lord gave John a word for our congregation, and he asked me if he could share it publicly. Because we had known each other in ministry, I trusted him completely and answered, "Absolutely!"

John stood up in front of everyone gathered for the dedication service and told them the Lord was saying we needed a new perspective about money. Like most churches moving into a new building, we were concerned about the rise in our monthly expenses. We had estimated that we were going to have a shortfall of $10,000 a month if we didn't see new money come in. However, John's word to us indicated that we no longer needed to worry about having enough, but rather should plan how to steward the incredible flow of resources the Lord would send us. He told us, "There won't be one month you will fall short. You will have all you need. Start praying now that God will expand your ability to handle the increase."

That was a pretty bold message! But within the year, his word came to pass. The Oaks had so much money we had to figure out what to do with it, just like the prophecy foretold. That was the start of my prophetic relationship with John and The Oaks.

It wasn't to be the last. Over the years, I've learned to trust John's heart, his integrity, and his prophetic voice. Because he had earned my confidence, I was willing to listen when God used him to tell me things—even things that rocked my world.

FROM JOHN . . .

I've known Scott for over twelve years. During this time, I've had a front row seat to watch him develop into a strong leader and an excellent pastor. Under his leadership, The Oaks has become a beacon of influence in our community.

Scott and I both came to the suburbs of Dallas in 2003. In fact, we became pastors of churches that are only about eight minutes apart. I began my work as the pastor of Freedom Fellowship International when Scott was named senior pastor at The Oaks Fellowship.

At first, we both flourished in ministry and our churches were growing rapidly. Scott and I enjoyed a deepening relationship. There was no doubt God was knitting our hearts together. I felt we were really becoming colaborers, and in a way, partners.

However, it wasn't long before I had to deal with serious issues in my own church. We didn't have a strong foundation of leadership, and we began to struggle. Our numbers plummeted. We were no longer the growing, vibrant church we once were. It was as if I could feel my church, and my dreams, slipping through my fingers.

The stress took its toll, and I struggled with the temptation to compare the incredible things going on at Scott's church with the lack of growth at mine. Money seemed to be pouring into The Oaks. Instead of praying about attendance and the budget (like I was), Scott and his board were struggling to be good stewards of the outpouring of God's blessings. God had used me in a mighty way to bring a strong word to The Oaks, but I couldn't change what was happening in my own church.

It became increasingly difficult for me to watch as The Oaks continued to thrive while our church declined. Everything Scott seemed to try at The Oaks was turning to gold. My jealousy caused me to shut down. I could feel my heart grow cold and distant toward the things of God. When I drove from Dallas to my home in Waxahachie, I had to drive by Scott's church. I couldn't even glance in that direction without being reminded of my own failures.

I was finally able to say to God, "I thought I was heading toward success, but I can see now that's not the case. Lord, I choose to follow You. I repent of the jealousy I've had in my heart toward Scott and The Oaks. I commit my life to following Your plan. Your will be done." This prayer was the beginning of my healing and deliverance from crippling jealousy. But would I have the courage to go through the rest of the healing process?

God challenged me with a bold question: "John, would you be willing to go to The Oaks in person and ask their forgiveness for your jealousy toward them?"

I called Scott to ask if I could come and speak to their prayer team. He gave his permission. In front of their whole team, I repented of the jealousy I felt in my heart toward their church and their pastor. God knew that the only way for me to be healed was for me to publicly ask their forgiveness.

It was time for me to get out of my own way and allow God to work through me more than ever before.

This act was both humbling and liberating. The fire of the experience helped me see that my problem was disobedience. My envy, self-pity, and doubts had been like poison. The antidote was humility and repentance. In hindsight, I recognize this painful experience was part of God's deeper work to prepare me for the future. In fact, He was about to call me to a much greater degree of obedience. It was time for me to get out of my own way and allow God to work through me more than ever before.

God gave me several other prophetic words for Scott and The Oaks. Each time, Scott and his leaders graciously listened and accepted what God told them through me. In 2012, the Lord gave me another message for my friend. That Thursday, He told me to ask Scott, "Will you give God one minute in your church service?" I could tell Scott was confused and shaken by the question, but I also knew he would carefully consider what the Lord was saying to him.

A few days later, on Saturday afternoon, I called Scott and asked him if I could come over to his office. I sensed that the Lord wanted us to follow up on our previous discussion. I arrived and went back to Scott's office. As soon as I walked in, we immediately began praying. After some time of prayer, I told him, "Scott, if you will give God a minute tomorrow, He will change things—really change things in ways you can't fathom. I have no idea what this is supposed to look like, but I know you have to be willing to try. Are you willing to trust Him?"

Scott looked at me. We both knew the seriousness of the moment. This was a big deal. God was upping the ante and asking for complete surrender. Neither of us knew what the change really meant. Scott is very organized. The services at The Oaks are exceptionally well prepared. Every aspect of the service is timed and runs like clockwork. People are coming on stage and off stage, coordinating set pieces, lights, sound, and special effects. There are a lot of overlapping parts to each service. To give up even one second's control would affect a lot of people. I could sense all those various details swirling around in Scott's head. I wondered, *Is Scott going to trust God in this?*

Scott looked up at me. I could tell he had made his decision. His face was set like flint. He solemnly and confidently told me, "John, I'm open to whatever God wants to do. God's way is far better than my way. He knows so much more than I know. This is a test . . . an opportunity. I'm open."

This book is about these two pivotal conversations, Scott's courage to implement the changes, and the way every pastor can invite the Spirit of God to radically transform him, the church's leadership, members and attenders, and ultimately, the entire community.

Note: We are including a few questions at the end of each chapter to stimulate your thinking, your prayers, and your conversations.

THINK ABOUT IT . . .

1. Why did you pick up this book? What do you hope to get out of it?

2. How do you think you would have responded if you had been Scott when John spoke a prophetic word to him?

3. Search your heart with humility and honesty, and consider whether jealousy or envy of another pastor, church, or ministry has in any way clouded your heart. Who is that pastor, or what is that church or ministry, and how will you face this problem?

CHAPTER 2

WHERE IT ALL BEGAN

After my conversations with John on Thursday morning and Saturday afternoon, I felt shattered. After the second meeting I went home to process all he had said to me. I wanted to be sure all this was from the Lord. That night I spent hours on my face before the Father. I asked Him for clarity, for wisdom, for direction. As I prayed, two things stood out. First, more than anything in the world, I wanted to please God. However, I also felt a deep sense of reluctance. I asked myself, *How did I get to this place . . . and why am I so afraid of giving the services back to God?*

HISTORY AND HESITATION

I love the Pentecostal church. I'm the son of a pastor, and I have a deep, abiding respect for those who have chosen to make serving this beautiful institution their life's work. All of the significant milestones of my own Christian journey have taken place at church events. I was saved at a church camp, filled with the Holy Spirit at a local camp meeting, called into ministry at youth camp, and anointed for full-time ministry on a church-sponsored mission trip to Arkansas. I'm a church guy down to my core!

I believe the church is a dynamic entity. But sometimes we get so caught up in our traditions that we become blind to creative approaches and uninterested in exploring new ways to worship and serve God. Some of our traditions, as valuable as they are, tend to keep us locked inside a box where God never intended us to stay.

In the 80s and 90s, I saw "the revival mentality" in many churches. Pastors and leaders of those churches believed God would lay His mighty hand on someone special to bring the great revival to our nation and the world. That special and anointed leader would hear from heaven and bring us a word from God in a brand new way. In the midst of citywide meetings, people would be touched and lives would be forever changed.

During the late twentieth century, God used this model to lead millions to faith in Christ and millions more to experience the fullness of the Spirit. But there was a downside. In many congregations, this revival mentality seemed to create an environment in which the gifts of the Spirit were possessed and practiced by just a few in the church. The rest seemed destined to watch in amazement. Oh, we *taught* that the gifts were for everyone, but we *acted* like only a few had the secrets of the mysterious and elusive gifts. It seemed that many congregations had a few individuals who were known throughout the church by their gifting. In any church, it wasn't unusual to notice the woman who always burst into tongues during the prayer meeting or the man who always brought a booming prophetic word—in King James English! It was their identity, their badge of honor, but instead of building people up, it often led to a painful and confusing division between the "haves" and the "have-nots."

In some cases, the exercise of the gifts became weird. I know because I saw it. When I was young, I didn't dare invite my friends to church because I was afraid someone was going to start dancing and screaming in tongues, or another person would stand up and give a harsh prophetic word against rock music, tattoos, and pierced body parts. But usually the problem was subtler: people were talking more about the gifts than marveling at the Giver. They may not have been taught about the nature and gifts of the Spirit. Or maybe they took their eyes off the wonder of God's amazing grace and tried to outdo each other in exercising spiritual gifts.

I remember a wise, elder pastor speaking to me about this problem. He said, "The problem with our generation is that we idolized the gifts more than we utilized the gifts."

I became frustrated with the self-indulgent revival meetings that bore little lasting fruit. The deep dissatisfaction I felt made me responsive to a new church strategy that was arriving on the scene. I started hearing of fast-growing churches that didn't revolve around a once-a-year revival mentality. They were called "seeker-friendly" churches. Unbelievers felt comfortable there, and they came in droves. These new churches were characterized by a genuine love for the lost. Their services were uplifting and encouraging. Gone was the desire to point out sin or stand in judgment of wrongdoing. The focus was more on the transforming power of God's grace than the fear of condemnation. The VIPs in every service weren't the "old guard" with their season-ticket seats in the same pews every Sunday. The VIPs at these new churches were the lost, the disenfranchised, and the new believers who felt welcomed and inspired. They showed up every time the church doors opened.

Some church leaders scoffed at churches like these and accused them of "being soft on the gospel." But most of the pastors I knew weren't soft on the gospel at all. They were bringing relevant messages, wrapped in practical application and real-time truth. They spoke in a common vernacular in a way people could grasp; they avoided awkward religious language. They called people to repentance and obedience, but not in a harsh, demanding tone. And they taught people how to grow in their faith. In our tradition, we had always taught the "what." These new churches were also teaching the "why" and "how."

SATURDAY NIGHT

When John confronted me with the prophetic word, I faced a dilemma. I still wholly believed in Pentecostal doctrine, but I had led the shift in our church toward a new, more "seeker-friendly" style of worship. My goal and strategy were to build a church where people were led well and loved well. Attendance at The Oaks had grown to about 2,500 using this model.

I knew there was awesome power in the gifts of the Holy Spirit, but I couldn't fathom how they could be effective in a church that tried to be relevant and seeker-friendly. The church's emphasis on tongues, in particular, left me wondering why more attention in many Pentecostal churches wasn't devoted to love and encouragement like I had seen in the seeker churches. I spoke in tongues every single day. The gift was (and is) a vital, ongoing part of my life, but I secretly wrestled with the fact that I would be very happy if we never had a public gift of tongues in our services again. I wanted our services to be known for love rather than speaking in tongues or powerful words of prophecy. John's prophetic word surfaced and heightened my dilemma.

As I prayed and studied, a vision took shape to marry these two divergent streams. With directed leadership training and discipleship, the sacred traditions of the Pentecostal doctrine could effectively reach out to the lost and disciple believers in a new and relevant way.

John's question on Thursday and Saturday seemed to come out of the blue, but I realized God had been preparing me for this moment. I knew something was missing. For a long time, I'd had a nagging sense that God had more for us in our worship. When I looked at people walking through our doors, I saw very different demographics—gray-haired couples and hipsters wearing skinny jeans, farm people who came in their pickups and city dwellers who drove their hybrids, those who carried seven-pound King James Bibles and others who used the ESV app on their smartphones. On top of all that, some in attendance had been steeped in years of traditional Pentecostal worship, and lots of others didn't know what the word *Pentecostal* meant. I had assumed we were touching all those people, but doubts now clouded my heart. I wanted to find a way to make our worship thoroughly Pentecostal and yet somehow connect spiritually, emotionally, and culturally with the new people at our church.

I wanted to find a way to make our worship thoroughly Pentecostal and yet somehow connect spiritually, emotionally, and culturally with the new people at our church.

On Saturday night following the two conversations with John, I was praying and preparing for my message the next morning. Suddenly the Lord whispered the same question John had asked, "Son, I want to do something in the service tomorrow that's different from what you're planning. Would you be okay with that?"

I stammered, "Uh, of course, Lord." After a few seconds, I added, "By the way, You're God. You don't have to ask my permission to do something in Your own service."

He replied, "Well, I figured I would ask since you've been putting the services together without Me and then asking Me to bless them. This week I thought it might be good if you just let Me lead the service the way I want, and it will already be blessed." (It seemed as if He and John had talked about me.)

It was one of those precious and threatening moments when years of assumptions explode in an instant. I had heard John, but now I was *really* listening to God. I answered, "Oh, God, I'm so sorry! Of course I want You to lead the services. What do You want me to do?"

The Lord told me simply, "Announce to the church that 'it's a new day' and that you're giving the services back to Me . . . and I'll do the rest."

"I'll do the rest"? What did *that* mean? Our team and I had always prayed to ask God's blessing on our services, but this was different. Planning and prayer have been and always will be integral parts of our preparation, but I realized I hadn't been listening carefully to the Spirit.

I had made too many assumptions about the way the service should go. Now, I was all ears.

A NEW DAY

Before our first service the next morning, I told our staff and worship team about my conversation with God. I took a deep breath and said, "Be ready for whatever God wants to do today. I'm going to explain that it's a new day for our church. Then we're going to stop the music and wait to hear a word from the Lord."

People filed in that morning and took their seats. Clayton Brooks, our worship pastor, led us in singing "Jesus, Jesus, Jesus. There's just something about that name." I sensed the presence of God, and He told me, "Now, son. It's time. Tell the people it's a new day."

I waved to Clayton to stop singing, and I walked to the front of the platform. I announced, "Friends, the Lord told me this is a new day for our church. He wants to be fully in control of our worship, and today I'm inviting Him to have His way with us. Now, let's be quiet before the Lord and allow Him to speak to us."

The silence wasn't awkward at all. There was a sense of anticipation, of wonder, of reverence. Then someone from the congregation spoke a prophetic word: "I am the Lord and I am leading this . . . I will not forsake you." Some of the non-charismatic folks may have thought we were performing a dramatic presentation, but we weren't performing anything. This word was God's assurance to me that I could trust Him to lead us.

At that moment I sensed the Lord whisper to me, "Son, you're the authority in this house. You're the pastor, so you must lead the way. You give a public expression of tongues right now, and you can trust Me to bring the interpretation."

After I boldly spoke in tongues, the Spirit prompted a brother to bring an interpretation. He said, "Why are you looking everywhere else for what you can only find in Me? Come to Me. Trust Me."

I explained to the congregation that according to 1 Corinthians 14:22, this word is for those who are searching for God. I told them, "The gift of tongues is a sign to you who are unbelievers so you can know that God is really in our midst. In this word, the secrets of your hearts are laid bare so you can repent of your sins and surrender your lives to Christ. God is using the gifts of tongues and interpretation of tongues as *a divine altar call*. If you sense this is God reaching out to you this morning, respond to Him in faith. He's reaching out to you and inviting you to come to Him. If you want to take His hand, come forward."

About forty people walked onto the stage to receive Christ. Many were kneeling. Some were weeping tears of relief and joy. They were meeting the Savior! I quickly realized some of the people in the room had no context for what they were experiencing. Before I prayed with those who were on the stage, I took a moment to explain how God uses spiritual gifts to draw people close to Him. I said, "Those of you who grew up Catholic or Baptist need to be thankful for your godly heritage, but if you ever exalt your heritage above the teaching of Scripture, you're wrong. And if you're Pentecostal or Charismatic, and you love the gifts so much that you exalt them above the leading of the Spirit, you're wrong. God meant for the gifts to be used to draw people closer to Him—just like we see happening this morning."

God meant for the gifts to be used to draw people closer to Him

After I prayed with those who were on the stage, I sensed God saying, "I'm not through. I have something for many more people this morning."

As the forty new believers continued praying on the platform, I turned to the congregation and announced, "Some of you have been Christians for a long time, but you sense the need to open your hearts to God. You want to say, 'Lord, I'm giving my life back to You. I've tried to run it, and I've failed. I want You to lead me.' If you sense God inviting you to return to Him, come forward, kneel before Him, and ask Him to take over."

About three hundred people came to the front to kneel and pray. I asked them to cup their hands in front of them and speak their fears into their hands. Then I told them to raise their fears up to heaven and let God have them. Many were deeply and visibly moved.

I explained that God had me cup my hands and speak my fears into them in the middle of the night earlier that week. I told them, "After a while, my arms got tired. I wanted to relax and drop them down, but God told me to go over to the wall and lean against it. He said, 'That's what you always do. You pull your fears back down onto yourself when you get tired and when you're hurting. This time, I want you to leave them with Me."

Clayton led the congregation in another song, and everyone went back to their seats. I preached the message God had given me, called "Waiting Time Isn't Wasting Time." It was from Isaiah 40:31:

> But those who hope in the Lord
>   will renew their strength.
> They will soar on wings like eagles;
>   they will run and not grow weary,
>   they will walk and not be faint.

This was the right passage for the right message at the right time for our church. I was waiting for the Lord to pour out His Spirit on me and lead me in a new day for our church. The word "renew" in this passage means to change clothes. Waiting isn't about time; it's about serving the One who deserves our attention and affection. We serve Him best if we take off our old clothes of selfishness and blindness and put on our new clothes of humility, love, and power. God will give us the power to fly over the difficulties in miraculous fashion, to run through the difficulties without getting weary and giving up, and sometimes to walk through the blistering desert of difficulties without fainting. God is looking for those of us who truly believe our lives are better with Him than without Him, that His way is better than ours, that His power is more effective than our efforts.

It was a magnificent worship service! But I had a problem. . . . Between services, I didn't know what to do. I wondered, *How do I get that to happen again? I can't just repeat it. That's not authentic. And if the next service isn't as good as the 9:30 one, the people who attend at 11:30 will feel upset.*

So I prayed, and I could almost see God smile and hear the hint of sarcasm in His voice, "Are you for real, Scott? Do you think you made those things happen? Just do what I told you to do, and I'll do what I want to do. Trust Me, son. Just trust Me."

I went in to begin the next service and prayed. I said, "God, please just let me know You're here, and assure me that You're going to move like You did in the earlier service." At that moment, Richard Miller, one of the elders, came over and touched my shoulder and said, "Pastor Scott, He's here!" I sensed God's smile as He told me, "Okay, go now and tell them it's a new day!"

And God showed up again.

During the next week, I heard story after story of people in the community who were touched by men and women who had heard the gospel at our worship services. God spoke to some in dreams. He miraculously healed the sick. Some people were baptized in the Holy Spirit and spoke in tongues without anyone praying for them.

A pastor from another church called during the week to tell me he had overheard two men talking as they repaired the toilet in his house. One of them was telling the other about our church service. He said, "Yesterday's service at our church was awesome! God changed me in a phenomenal way."

The other man asked, "What do you mean?"

He explained, "Before my wife and I went to church, God was really dealing with me about pride. He said, 'Son, you need to stop being so stubborn. You need to humble yourself. Bow your knee to Me.' I told my wife on the way to church that if the pastor gave us a chance to bow to the Lord, I was going to do it. Yesterday in church, Pastor Scott told us, 'It's a new day,' and he spoke out in tongues, and another guy interpreted it. It made me mad. I didn't believe in that stuff! Then Pastor Scott said, 'You need to bow your knee to the Lord and follow Him with all your heart.' That was it. That was the word God had been speaking to me already about my stubbornness and pride. I went forward, spoke my fears into my hands, and let them go. I lifted my hands to the

Lord and began to speak in tongues! I was so shocked that I put my hands over my mouth, but the spiritual words kept coming. When I got home, I apologized to my wife for how I had been treating her. This morning, I got up early to pray. I want God to make me a better man, a better husband, and a better worker. God is changing me! Wow!"

A new day had dawned on that man's family, on countless others, and on our church!

That Sunday and the following week were incredible, but what about the future? How did God want us to steward the moving of His Spirit in our services in the coming weeks, months, and years? Instead of trying to figure it out on my own, I thought I would ask God to give me directions. (I learn slowly, but eventually I learn a lesson or two.) I'll explain more about that in Chapter 6, "Rules of Engagement."

MY HEART, MY HOPE

Time-honored Pentecostal expressions of faith don't have to remain in the same packaging we used decades ago. Altar calls aren't the only place and time when God changes lives and baptizes believers in the Spirit. As the Holy Spirit leads us, we can create a new culture that is totally Pentecostal in values and gifts, and yet thoroughly contemporary to relate to the spiritually hungry seekers who attend our services.

Our fellowship of churches has a long and storied history of letting the Spirit of God flow in our services and through our lives. My hope is that we continue to live with the same heart that Donald Gee described in his book, *Toward Pentecostal Unity*. He wrote, "We ought not enjoy deep emotion at the expense of shallow thinking. 'I will pray with the Spirit but I will pray with the understanding also' is the scriptural way of putting it. The three golden strands of order, faith, and experience need weaving into the one cord that cannot quickly be broken. A Pentecostal revival in the fullest measure will not stress one at the expense of the others but will manifest a shining witness to all three."[1]

The practices we use at The Oaks are the result of much prayer and Bible study. We are motivated by love for every person who walks through the doors of our church—the old and the young, the traditional and the hip. We want all of them to be inspired and challenged by the truth, love, and power found in Jesus Christ. We're thrilled to have the gifts of the Spirit at work among us. For a long time, we've allowed the gifts to flow in our private prayer meetings, but now we're introducing hundreds (even thousands) of people to the gifts in public worship so that Christ is exalted and souls are saved.

This is a day to rejoice! God is moving in the hearts of His people. For too long, I assumed I played the central role in planning and orchestrating our worship experiences. I carried the burden like a heavy weight on my shoulders. But finally, God got my attention and asked me to serve Him instead of hoping He would serve and bless me. And now

I don't feel any pressure—except the responsibility to seek His face and His Word. When we seek His face, He delights to reveal himself to us. The promise of His presence, power, and love isn't only for private prayer and devotions. God wants to show up in our public worship, too.

The work of God isn't limited to Pentecostal traditions *or* modern worship. If we listen to the Spirit and follow His lead, God will give us the grace to be both Pentecostal *and* contemporary. He is our great King and loving Savior, and He wants to have His way in our lives and our leadership. I'm all in, and I hope you are, too.

It's amazing what God can do when we give Him our hearts, our lives, and our worship services and trust Him to lead everything. Before we examine the structure and process of how to reframe our worship services and corporate prayer, we need to take a good look at the biblical foundations of our new day.

THINK ABOUT IT . . .

1. Describe your denominational history. How have the traditions helped to give you structure and substance? How have they limited creativity and the flow of the Spirit?

2. How have you responded to the modern "seeker friendly" models? What about them is worthwhile? What elements are suspect in your mind?

3. Are you anxious about the manifestations of the Holy Spirit taking place in your church services? Take time to carefully consider your answer. What would give you confidence?

4. What did it mean for Scott to announce, "It's a new day" at The Oaks? What would it mean for you to have a new day at your church?

SECTION 2

THE FOUNDATION

(SCOTT'S VOICE)

CHAPTER 3

EVERYBODY GETS A FLAME

My friend Jim Hennesy is the pastor of Trinity Church in Cedar Hill, Texas. He was asked to speak at a conference I attended. I had just come in and sat down as he announced the title of his talk: "Reclaiming Pentecost: Everybody Gets a Flame." It was one of those moments when a few words have the power of a sledgehammer. I thought, *That's it! The power of the Spirit isn't reserved for a few. It's for everybody!*

Instantly, I remembered Jesus' baptism when the Holy Spirit descended like a dove and rested on Him (John 1:32). That moment in Jesus' ministry parallels the believers' experience of the Spirit descending on them at Pentecost. Before that event in Jerusalem, however, Jesus explained the role of the Spirit. On the night He was betrayed, He told His disciples something that must have confused them at the time:

> "Very truly I tell you, whoever believes in me will do the works I have been doing, and they will do even

> greater things than these, because I am going to the Father. And I will do whatever you ask in my name, so that the Father may be glorified in the Son. You may ask me for anything in my name, and I will do it." (John 14:12–14)

I can almost hear the disciples whispering to each other, "What's He talking about? Us? *Greater things* than He has done? We've watched Him cleanse lepers, restore sight to the blind, heal the sick, feed the multitudes, and raise the dead! How in the world can we do more than that?"

Without missing a beat, Jesus gave them the answer: "I will ask the Father, and he will give you another advocate to help you and be with you forever—the Spirit of truth" (John 14:16–17). A few minutes later, Jesus told them, "I am the vine; you are the branches. If you remain in me and I in you, you will bear much fruit; apart from me you can do nothing" (John 15:5).

The fruit Jesus was talking about isn't only personal spiritual experience. It's that, of course, but it's much, much more. Jesus came to give, to love, to sacrifice, and to make a difference in the lives of any who would listen. We have a far bigger purpose in life than stimulating, self-indulgent, personal experiences. The Spirit's goal is to transform us from the inside out so that we increasingly have Jesus' heart for people.

EVERYONE GETS A PURPOSE

Many people, including many Christians, struggle to find their purpose in life. They wander from this activity to that one, this group to some other, this church to that one. Many of them think there's a secret key to unlock the mysteries of meaning for their lives. But the meaning of our lives is no secret; it's on page after page of the Bible.

One of the problems is that many of those who come to church each week assume God exists to help them fulfill *their* agendas. But God isn't our employee. He's the King. The things the world values can't give us true meaning. They don't challenge us to bring out our best for God's glory. The world's purposes are self-serving, not self-sacrificing. How do we know what we value most? It's what we think about when we have spare time, what we daydream about, where we spend our time, and how we invest our money. The Lord spoke through Jeremiah:

The things the world values can't give us true meaning. They don't challenge us to bring out our best for God's glory.

> This is what the LORD says:
> "Let not the wise boast of their wisdom

or the strong boast of their strength
or the rich boast of their riches,
but let the one who boasts boast about this:
that they have the understanding to know me,
that I am the LORD, who exercises kindness,
justice and righteousness on earth,
for in these I delight,"
declares the LORD. (Jer. 9:23–24)

The Lord delights in our knowing and loving Him, and then, out of the overflow of that love, pouring ourselves out in kindness, justice, and righteousness to everyone around us.

Jesus explained this dual purpose in what are commonly known as "the Great Commandment" and "the Great Commission." An expert in the Mosaic law asked Jesus to identify the greatest of all the Old Testament commandments. Jesus replied, "'Love the Lord your God with all your heart and with all your soul and with all your mind.' This is the first and greatest commandment. And the second is like it: 'Love your neighbor as yourself.' All the Law and the Prophets hang on these two commandments" (Matt. 22:37–40).

What does it mean to love people? To Jesus, it meant many things. He made sure His followers didn't miss the point of His coming to earth. Only hours after Jesus' final instructions to His disciples, He was falsely accused, unfairly tried, wrongly convicted, and unjustifiably sentenced to death. With His crucifixion it seemed that evil had won, but in reality it was the greatest demonstration of the purposes of God in the history of humankind! The resurrection proved that victory had been won through the Messiah's sacrifice, blood, and death. For the next forty days, Jesus appeared many times to His followers—to as many as 500 at one time. Then, when it was time for Him to leave, He led the apostles out to a hill and gave them the Great Commission:

> "All authority in heaven and on earth has been given to me. Therefore go and make disciples of all nations, baptizing them in the name of the Father and of the Son and of the Holy Spirit, and teaching them to obey everything I have commanded you. And surely I am with you always, to the very end of the age." (Matt. 28:18–20)

During this conversation, the disciples asked Jesus, "Lord, are you at this time going to restore the kingdom to Israel" (Acts 1:6)? In effect, His reply was, "You guys don't get it. Yes, I am setting up My kingdom, but not in the way you expect. I'm going to set it up *through you*, and I'm sending My Spirit to equip and empower you."

In His last words before ascending to the Father, Jesus gave them a mandate, assurances, and instructions. The mandate was far broader than they had ever imagined: to make disciples in every nation on the globe. It had been hard enough to minister in Israel, but God's love spills out to every tribe, tongue, people, and nation. In other words, there are no boundaries of race, gender, nationality, politics, age, or religion. Jesus loves them all. As our hearts are knit with His, we will love them, too.

Jesus knew His followers well. He knew they were a fearful bunch . . . people just like us. So He gave them three assurances:

- He has all authority in heaven and on earth. His kingdom, His power, and His presence know no limits.
- He was leaving, but He promised His perpetual presence through the Holy Spirit. We are never beyond His reach, His love, or His authority.
- He will give us the power to do whatever He asks us to do. He never said it would be easy, but He promised to give us the power we need in all circumstances.

Jesus told them to wait in Jerusalem for "what the Father promised," the baptism in the Holy Spirit (Acts 1:4–5). To make sure they understood, He explained, "But you will receive power when the Holy Spirit comes on you; and you will be my witnesses in Jerusalem, and in all Judea and Samaria, and to the ends of the earth" (Acts 1:8). Jesus ascended forty days after Passover (Acts 1:3), and His disciples waited in Jerusalem another ten days, until the feast of

Pentecost, for the outpouring of the Spirit. Jesus told them to wait in order to be filled with power, and that's all we need to do as well.

EVERYONE GETS THE POWER

God's mandate and assurances in our lives are the same that Jesus gave His followers on that hillside twenty centuries ago. The Great Commandment and the Great Commission aren't reserved for pastors and missionaries. Whether people are nurses, masons, stay-at-home parents, attorneys, or in any other career, they have been given the high calling of representing the King of Kings in their circles of influence, starting with their family and friends, then their communities, and on to the farthest reaches of the earth. But they don't have to try to make disciples alone. They have God's magnificent assurances of His presence, authority, and power.

Pentecost is the Greek name for the ancient Jewish celebration known as the Feast of Weeks, also called the day of the firstfruits (Num. 28:26) or the Festival of Harvest or Festival of Reaping (Ex. 23:16). For centuries before Jesus walked the earth, the Jewish people celebrated the Feast of Weeks, which was observed exactly fifty days after the Sabbath after Passover. Two things marked the event: the celebration of God's giving the law to Moses and a "first fruit" offering from the summer harvest—a sign to God that they believed He would provide all they needed for the year.

Both Passover and Pentecost focused on the two main aspects of God's covenant with His people: love and law. Each annual Passover meal was a reminder of how God had spared their lives in Egypt the night the angel of death descended to kill the firstborn in every household without lamb's blood on the doorposts. The sacrifice of a lamb in every Hebrew home was a symbol of God's sacrificial love, which was also emphasized in the Exodus by God's holy presence with His people in the pillars of fire and cloud. In the following centuries, similar sacrifices in the tabernacle and the temple reminded people of the ongoing love of God.

During the Feast of Weeks, fifty days after Passover, the people remembered the Law of Moses given at Mount Sinai. In conjunction with their firstfruits offering, which acknowledged God's loving provision for them, they also read the first five books of the Bible, the Pentateuch, and thanked God for His Word.

We, too, need to acknowledge both law and love in our relationships with God. The law gives us directions to obey God, yet it also reveals our desperate need for a Savior because we realize we cannot keep

The law gives us directions to obey God, yet it also reveals our desperate need for a Savior because we realize we cannot keep its requirements.

its requirements. (See Gal. 3:24 and Rom. 3:23.) Knowing that people were unable to adhere to the standards of the Law, God sent His Son to deal once and for all with the problem of sin. Law and love—we need to understand both of them if we're going to walk with God.

Pentecost (Feast of Weeks) was a busy day in Jerusalem. It was one of the three times each year that all able-bodied men were supposed to make the journey to Jerusalem (Ex. 23:14–17; Deut. 16:16). But on the first day of Pentecost after the death of Jesus, His followers were in the city with a special sense of anticipation. Fifty days earlier the apostles had celebrated the Passover with Jesus, and He had told them to stay in the city "until you are clothed with power from on high" (Luke 24:49; see also Acts 1:4–5). They probably didn't understand it fully, but they were waiting for the Holy Spirit's presence and power. A group of 120 believers was waiting and praying in an upper room. They wanted to be ready when the time came.

In ancient times, Moses had gone up to Mount Sinai to get the Law *to show people how* to live, but Jesus went up to heaven to send the Spirit *to empower people* to live. Luke, the historian of the early church, tells us what happened:

> When the day of Pentecost came, they were all together in one place. Suddenly a sound like the blowing of a violent wind came from heaven and filled the whole house where they were sitting. They

> saw what seemed to be tongues of fire that separated and came to rest on each of them. All of them were filled with the Holy Spirit and began to speak in other tongues as the Spirit enabled them. (Acts 2:1–4)

Who was involved in this event? Not one or two of them. Not some of them. Not the higher or lower classes of them. Not just the apostles. "All of them were filled with the Holy Spirit and began to speak in other tongues."

The people listening and watching were amazed. They were from all over the Roman world, speaking many different ethnic languages. Those 120 plain, unschooled Jewish people were "declaring the wonders of God" (Acts 2:11) in languages they had never learned. The tongues Luke describes in this event were consistent with the nature of tongues described by Paul in his first letter to the Corinthians. The 120 were proclaiming praise to God, not preaching. The convicting word came from Peter. His prophetic message was a powerful blend of law and love, of judgment and grace, of warning and invitation. On the spot, 3,000 people trusted in Jesus, God's Messiah, to pay for their sins and give them new life! They were the firstfruit offering to God on the Day of Pentecost.

THE SOUND OF HEAVEN

When the Holy Spirit came upon the believers in their upper room, it wasn't a silent moment. Luke tells us it sounded like the wind from a thunderstorm or a tornado or a hurricane—"a rushing mighty wind" (Acts 2:2, NKJV) filling the whole house. What would the sound of heaven be like in our churches today? Is it even possible that the Spirit might want to come among us in this way? The disciples were praying when the sound enveloped them. The same kind of thing can happen when we pray fervently in the Spirit.

I began to pray that our church would be filled with the sound of heaven. Can you imagine being in a room with a group of passionate, committed believers who all want—more than anything else in the world—to experience the purpose, power, and presence of God? They would be people who aren't ashamed of the Spirit's work in them and among them; people who aren't hesitant to cry out to God to do what only He can do; people consumed with the love of God for the people praying next to them, the people who normally annoy them, the people who look different, act different, and vote differently; people who live in the next bedroom, across the street, or on the other side of the world.

It's possible. John and I have been a part of a group of people who regularly hear the sound of heaven as we pray. It's the sound of the Spirit speaking to us, through us, and in us—and it can't be contained. We can worship God in a way that invites the angels to join in! The heavenly hosts can fill the place with songs of praise as they listen to our songs of redemption.

Many of us have right doctrines, but our hearts are reserved. We say we've given our whole hearts to Jesus, but our prayers are routine and our praise is tepid. When you pray, are you aware that you're connecting with the One who spoke and the galaxies were flung into space? Does it amaze you that the Son of God stepped out of the splendor of heaven to set foot on earth as a servant to live and die for those who ignored or despised Him? If there's no wonder, there's no real praise. If we're not amazed, we'll hold something back. If we're not stunned by the grace of God for sinners like us, we will serve halfheartedly or only in order to be noticed by people.

Some might say, "I'm distracted by all the worries and demands of life." Nonsense. Certainly, we all have concerns and demands. We are fallen people who live in a fallen world, but we have a connection with the greatest love, the greatest power, and the greatest purpose the world has ever known! When He amazes us, our distractions fade away. We can look at all our worries through the lens of faith in the only One

We are fallen people who live in a fallen world, but we have a connection with the greatest love, the greatest power, and the greatest purpose the world has ever known!

who has ultimate authority and compassion. And in Him, we can relax and trust.

Pastors, we're not immune to a watered-down passion for God. A new day begins with us. We can't expect our people to marvel at God's goodness and greatness if our hearts aren't thrilled with Him. We need to cast out all distractions, fear, and pride and replace them with wonder, praise, and faith. As we become less inhibited, our people will notice. We'll be the fuse that lights the dynamite of supernatural power in their lives. Then, together, we can cry out to God with a loud voice and full hearts for the Spirit of God to come among us, fill us, and empower us to fulfill His agenda for us and for the world. When this happens, we will hear the sound of heaven among us.

All of us need models to help us get a picture of what God wants to do among us. John has helped me experience the sound of heaven as he and I have prayed together. It's wonderful! I had another example when I attended a conference and heard Pastor Niko Njotorahardjo, from Jakarta, Indonesia as he spoke about prayer at his church. He didn't speak much English, but he brought a video of a prayer meeting. As we watched, thousands of people in his church stood to their feet and with full voices cried out to the Lord. It was incredible. It must have been like that in the upper room on Pentecost. I closed my eyes and lifted my hands. I hoped it would never stop. I felt like I was at the door of heaven listening to saints and angels sing and pray to the Lord. With that kind of spirit, people are willing to do anything for the King! But that experience isn't reserved for a moment in the lives of 120 people two millennia ago or in a huge church in Indonesia today.

The Spirit of God is waiting for His people—and especially His pastors and church leaders—to invite Him to invade our hearts, our leadership, our prayer meetings, and our worship services so powerfully that it sounds like a mighty rushing wind. It's the sound of heaven . . . can you hear it?

FIRE FROM HEAVEN

Fire is a powerful and persistent metaphor in the Bible, from the burning bush to the burnt offerings of sacrifices to the "consuming fire" of God's judgment. In the events of that first Pentecost of the church, tongues of fire were symbolic of the Spirit's presence and power. Fire has two primary purposes: to purify and to empower.

The fire of the Spirit illumines the dark places of our lives and reveals our blind spots, secret sins, and long-ignored pride. The Spirit's work to reveal is only the first part of His work to purify. When we confess and repent, the Spirit burns away the dross from our lives and leaves us pure and forgiven before God. This will happen in an ultimate way at the judgment seat of Christ when the actions of all believers will pass through the purifying fire, burning up selfish ambitions and leaving the pure gold, silver, and precious stones of our love for God and faithfulness to His calling (1 Cor. 3:10–15).

But fire also is a source of incredible power. We use it in our homes, our vehicles, our cooking, and in many other aspects of life. The Spirit didn't come upon those in the upper room to make them happy and self-absorbed. He came to empower them to fulfill God's bold calling to represent Him in every situation and in every corner of the earth. The disciples in the upper room were united in prayer and focused on God's Word. That's the fuel of the Spirit's power. When we aren't reading, studying, and responding to the Word of God, we have no fuel to burn.

God's calling isn't reserved for a few super-saints. It's for all of us. What would it look like if everyone in our churches were on fire for God? But first, we who are leaders need to ask ourselves: What are we on fire for? What is our driving passion? Or has the fire dwindled to a flicker? Too often, our passions are divided. It's God *and* money, God *and* prestige, God *and* power, God *and* comfort. A day will come when God's fire will purge away all the "ands" from our lives. Let's not wait for it to happen later. We can invite the Spirit to purify us and empower us today to be fully His.

All of us, even the best among us, can drift. That's why Paul wrote Timothy, his protégé, "For this reason I remind you to fan into flame the gift of God, which is in you through the laying on of my hands" (2 Tim. 1:6).

ALL IN LOVE

The Spirit of God doesn't put people on a power trip. His power is never used to intimidate or dominate. He is exquisitely kind and tender. He grieves over our harshness and bitterness. The Spirit's presence in our lives always produces the fruit of "love, joy, peace, forbearance, kindness, goodness, faithfulness, gentleness and self-control" (Gal. 5:22–23). The gifts of the Spirit are fertilizer that helps people grow spiritual fruit.

The Corinthian Christians must have been much like many of our church congregations—more than a little off-target when it comes to understanding spiritual life! They assumed they could use the Spirit's power, and all the sign gifts, to pad their résumés and gain prestige among their peers. Paul disabused them of this notion. We often use "the love chapter" in weddings, but 1 Corinthians 13 is actually a severe corrective for the Christians in Corinth. Paul told them bluntly:

> If I speak in the tongues of men or of angels, but do not have love, I am only a resounding gong or a clanging cymbal. If I have the gift of prophecy and can fathom all mysteries and all knowledge, and if I have a faith that can move mountains, but do not have love, I am nothing. If I give all I possess to the poor and give over my body to hardship that I may

> boast, but do not have love, I gain nothing. (1 Cor. 13:1–3)

Paul said that God is irritated with people who speak in tongues but aren't filled with love. He isn't impressed with those who have profound spiritual insights but aren't compassionate. He is annoyed with those who demonstrate miraculous spiritual power but don't care about others. He shrugs when He sees dramatic sacrifice that isn't motivated by genuine love for people.

Love, Paul explained, was very different from what the Corinthians had demonstrated (and the problems he had addressed earlier in his letter).

> Love is patient, love is kind. It does not envy, it does not boast, it is not proud. It does not dishonor others, it is not self-seeking, it is not easily angered, it keeps no record of wrongs. Love does not delight in evil but rejoices with the truth. It always protects, always trusts, always hopes, always perseveres. Love never fails. (1 Cor. 13:4–8)

Demonstrations of the gifts aren't the ultimate benchmark of spiritual life. They should reflect the love of God poured into us and overflowing into the lives of others. Without that, we're just making noise. At The Oaks, I'm not clearing the stage and changing our model of ministry to highlight the spiritual gifts of tongues, prophecy, healing, and miracles. All of those things didn't matter to Paul—and they don't matter to me—if they don't deepen our love for God, for our families, for our neighbors, and for every other person we meet. The test of loyalty to God isn't the gifts; it's kindness, tenderness, and compassion.

The test of loyalty to God isn't the gifts; it's kindness, tenderness, and compassion.

OPEN HEARTS

At the conference where I heard Pastor Niko speak, the people planning the event asked me to share what God is doing at The Oaks to "clear the stage" for the Spirit to work. I told them how God had been moving in my relationship with John and in our church services, and I explained that it was "a new day" at our church. I only spoke a few minutes, and I closed with a prayer for the leaders in the room. I asked God to do this kind of thing in churches around the world and convict our hearts of pride, fear, and compulsive control as we surrender ourselves into His strong, wise, and loving hands.

As we prayed, the Spirit of God fell in the room. I have seldom sensed Him so powerfully present. The leaders of the event stopped the program, and we prayed for an hour and a half. One of the ladies gave a prophetic word about our church and me. She said, "Pastor Scott, God has given you a great responsibility. He has given you stewardship of a deep well, a deep well of His Spirit. The well has been uncapped, and He has chosen you to steward the well for His people."

The next morning I received an email from a lady who hasn't attended our church in about three years. She wrote:

> Hey Pastor Scott,
> I had a dream the other night with you and Jenni in it. I wanted to share what I sensed God was telling me. My husband and I drove up to what we knew was the church you pastored, and we saw you outside in the front, working on its well. Jenni was standing on the front porch. It was more like a very nice house with ornate décor. You had a very concerned look on your face. You were working, but you stopped to talk to us long enough to tell us that you had to get the well working again. I sensed the Lord say to you that He sees your heart for the deep and simple things in Him and your desire for the living water of His Spirit. I believe He has more to say to you on this, so I bless you as you pursue His word for you.

God showed both of these ladies on the same night, thousands of miles from each other, that He was uncapping a deep well of His Spirit at The Oaks. He has given me stewardship of the well. I—and the other leaders of our church—have the responsibility to receive all God wants to pour into our well, and then to use the deep well of His love, power, and truth to change countless lives in our community and throughout the world.

If you're a pastor or church leader, God wants to uncap the deep well of His Spirit in your life and your church. And He wants you to be the steward of His living water.

Pastors, it's not all about you. You aren't the keeper of the flame; you're the lighter for everyone else's flame. In the greeting in Peter's second letter, he addressed all of his readers: "To those who through the righteousness of our God and Savior Jesus Christ have received a faith as precious as ours: Grace and peace be yours in abundance through the knowledge of God and of Jesus our Lord" (2 Peter 1:1–2).

Every believer has a faith as precious as Peter's, Paul's, yours, or mine. In Jesus' great prayer, He says that all believers have the same purpose that infused Christ's life: "As you sent me into the world, I have sent them into the world" (John 17:18). And He prayed that each of us would be amazed that the Father loves us as much as He loves His Son: "I have made you known to them, and will continue to make you known in order that the love you have for me may be in them and that I myself may be in them" (John 17:26). There are no second-class citizens in God's kingdom. It's our privilege and responsibility as pastors and leaders to teach, inspire, and direct people to fulfill their awesome, God-given calling.

If spiritual leaders try to hoard the flame, the people in the church will criticize them or idolize them. Neither option works for me! None of us wants to be criticized, but it's tempting to be seen as "an awesome prophet," a "holy man (or woman) of God." If pastors don't see their main job as spreading the fire of the Spirit to every person they know, the Great Commandment won't be fulfilled because people will be judging instead of loving, and the Great Commission won't be fulfilled because people will be self-absorbed instead of reaching out to share the greatest story ever told.

Pastors and missionaries aren't an elite group that has the flame of the Spirit. Everyone in your church has a flame, and God wants to use you to ignite each one. Everyone in your church has a divine purpose, and God wants to use you to direct them to the right places of effectiveness. Everyone in your church has the power of the Spirit, and God wants to use you to unleash them.

When this begins to happen, nothing will stop the rushing wind. You will hear the sound of heaven . . . in your heart, in your prayer services, and in your church. There's nothing like it.

THINK ABOUT IT . . .

1. What happens in a church that has a division between the "haves" and the "have-nots" regarding spiritual gifts?

2. What does it take to hear the sound of heaven in your heart, in your prayer services, and in your church?

3. What will it cost you to hear that sound?

4. Describe the specific steps you will take so that you and your church hear the sound of heaven.

CHAPTER 4

SPIRIT-LED LIVING

I was with a good friend when God called him to be a pastor. It was a glorious moment. When he started his church, I had been a pastor for about nine years. I was the pro; he was the rookie—at least, that's the way I saw it at the time. He called me every few weeks to ask my advice about all kinds of situations he faced. I was glad to help.

My friend's church grew like crazy. They opened a second campus where they had over 1,000 people the first week. Eighteen months later, they opened a third campus, and they had over 1,500 people on the opening Sunday.

Funny thing... I wasn't as glad to help any more. It wasn't like he needed me! Our church had hit a plateau. His church was booming; ours had fizzled. I tried to stop thinking about it, but when I heard news about his church, it ate my lunch. I was discouraged, and to be honest, a bit angry—not at my friend, but at God. I wondered why God wasn't blessing our church. I thought about opening a second campus. I thought about a lot of things—most of them weren't very positive!

I've always struggled with comparison, with self-promotion, and with competition with other pastors, even my best friends. During the difficult months after my friend's third campus opened, I met often with John Bates. He kept reminding me that I needed to stop comparing The Oaks with the ABCs of other churches: attendance, buildings, and cash. He said, "Scott, it's more like golf. It's just you and God on the course. Don't think about any other players. Just play your game."

I wish comparison was the only struggle in my life. It's not. I wrestle with exaggeration, image management, manipulation, and plenty of other stuff. I wanted to experience freedom, joy, and relief from all those inner conflicts. I knew plenty of principles and techniques. I taught a bunch of them, but I didn't feel free. I sometimes wondered if it was even possible to be really free.

The promises of God are magnificent, and the Spirit's presence is awesome, but we live in the awkward tension between the "already" and the "not yet."

REAL STRUGGLES, REAL HOPE

The promises of God are magnificent, and the Spirit's presence is awesome, but we live in the awkward tension between the "already" and the "not yet." Many of God's promises have already been fulfilled in us and for us, but the complete consummation of His promises won't happen until we're with Him in the new heaven and new earth. Until then, Spirit-led living is a struggle, a fight, a war between opposing forces.

The apostle Paul understood that fact very well. His letter to the Romans teaches God's truth about all kinds of crucial topics: heaven and hell, creation, judgment and forgiveness, justification, sanctification, the work of grace, the role of the Spirit, our adoption into the family of God, the connection to the Old Testament, law and government, relating to difficult people, and many other issues. A pastor could spend ten years teaching from Paul's letter and never plumb the depths of it.

Almost right in the middle of this glorious writing, Paul shares his own struggles. As a pastor, he teaches the glorious truth of God's forgiveness, power, and hope, but he also is painfully honest about his failures. We might not want to look beneath the surface of Paul's life, but he gives us no option. He paints the ugly picture in a long chapter. Earlier, he taught about the wonder of God's grace in Jesus Christ, and he explained that the Law is effective to reveal our sins. Then he admits to his personal struggle. In the seventh chapter, he confesses, "I do not understand what I do. For what I want to do I do not do, but what I hate I do. And if I do what I do not want to do, I agree that the law is good. . . . For I do not do the good I want to do, but the evil I do not want to do—this I keep on doing" (Rom. 7:15–16, 19).

We can feel his exasperation at the end of his confession when he exclaims, "What a wretched man I am! Who will rescue me from this body that is subject to death" (Rom. 7:24)?

I'm so glad the letter doesn't end there, because Paul then goes into one of the most hopeful, powerful, and inspiring chapters in the Bible! The link is found at the end of chapter 7 and the opening verses of chapter 8:

> Thanks be to God, who delivers me through Jesus Christ our Lord! So then, I myself in my mind am a slave to God's law, but in my sinful nature a slave to the law of sin. Therefore, there is now no condemnation for those who are in Christ Jesus, because through Christ Jesus the law of the Spirit who gives life has set you free from the law of sin and death. (Rom. 7:25–8:2)

Many Christians, including many pastors, are still living on Mount Sinai. They know God's righteous requirements as spelled out in the Law, and they try very hard to keep them all. Ironically, the harder they try, the more they realize how far short they fall! Like Paul, they cry out for help! But unlike Paul, many of them just put their heads down and try harder. It never works. In a sermon series on "Practical Grace," Pastor Tim Keller explains that walking in the Spirit isn't just about having a "morally restrained heart, but a supernaturally changed heart."[2]

In the eighth chapter of Romans, Paul explained how God supernaturally transforms our hearts. God has given four distinct blessings to every believer:

Forgiveness and freedom

For believers, there is "no condemnation" because Jesus has already paid the price for our sins. We are free from the punishment of the Law because Jesus has already fulfilled all its requirements, and we are "in Him" (Rom. 8:1).

The power and presence of the Spirit

Paul explains that the Holy Spirit has taken up residence in every believer. He empowers us to "put sin to death" (Rom. 8:13) in our lives, and He prays for us when we are too confused or weak to know how to pray (Rom. 8:26–27).

Assurance and sonship

Amazingly, we have been adopted into God's family—not as stepchildren who are barely tolerated, but equal with Christ, "co-heirs" with Him. The Holy Spirit "testifies with our spirit that we are God's children" (Rom. 8:16) to assure us that we belong to Him. In *Knowing God,* J. I. Packer explains,

> God . . . loves us with the same steadfast affection with which He eternally loves His beloved only-begotten. There are no distinctions of affection in

the divine family. We are all loved just as fully as Jesus is loved. It is like a fairy story—the reigning monarch adopts waifs and strays to make princes of them—but praise God, it is not a fairy story: it is hard and solid fact, founded on the bedrock of free and sovereign grace. This, and nothing less than this, is what adoption means. No wonder that John cries, "Behold, what manner of love . . . !" When once you understand adoption, your heart will cry the same.[3]

Confidence in God's purposes and plan

Paul recognized that we face many confusing, disappointing, disturbing situations. Our tendency is to walk away or shake our fists at God because we assume He has let us down. Not so, Paul assures us. We can be confident that God is always at work for His glory and our good. Paul wrote, "And we know that in all things God works for the good of those who love him, who have been called according to his purpose" (Rom. 8:28).

We can be confident that God is always at work for His glory and our good.

As a good pastor, Paul went to great lengths to assure his readers, then and now, that God's love is everlasting—it will never fail. He asked and answered a series of questions—ones that anyone who has wrestled with Romans 7 would ask—and he concluded that nothing, "in all creation, will be able to separate us from the love of God that is in Christ Jesus our Lord" (Rom. 8:39).

Similarly, the apostle John assures us that the foundations of God's love will never be shaken. Many of us, even leaders who have read the Bible many times, still secretly believe our performance dictates God's verdict of our acceptance or rejection. That's why we're so driven to prove ourselves, and we're so shaken when we fail in any way. But God's verdict of forgiveness and acceptance comes first, *killing* performance. This way, we obey as beloved sons and daughters who delight to please our Father, and when we fail, we don't have to be terrified. We can be honest with Him and come running back because we know we're loved, forgiven, and accepted through the blood of Jesus. "Know" was an important word to John. It wasn't *think* or *hope* or *guess*. He wrote,

> This is how we know that we live in him and he in us: He has given us of his Spirit. And we have seen and testify that the Father has sent his Son to be the Savior of the world. If anyone acknowledges that Jesus is the Son of God, God lives in them and they in God. And so we know and rely on the love God has for us. . . . There is no fear in love. But perfect love drives out fear, because fear has to do with punishment. The one who fears is not made perfect in love. (1 John 4:13–16, 18)

We don't have to lie about our real struggles. Why? Because we have real hope in God's unconditional, magnificent, cleansing, powerful love. When we're convinced of this truth, we draw close to Him, and the Holy Spirit guides our steps. That's a Spirit-led life.

FIGHT TO WIN

In his letter to the Galatians, Paul described the spiritual conflict between the flesh, our natural selfishness, and the Spirit:

> You, my brothers and sisters, were called to be free. But do not use your freedom to indulge the flesh; rather, serve one another humbly in love. . . . So I say, walk by the Spirit, and you will not gratify the desires of the flesh. For the flesh desires what is contrary to the Spirit, and the Spirit what is contrary to the flesh. They are in conflict with each other, so that you are not to do whatever you want. But if you are led by the Spirit, you are not under the law. (Gal. 5:13, 16–18)

God has created us triune beings, somewhat like the three persons of the Trinity. We are body, soul, and spirit. The conflict among these parts, Paul explained, is where we fight against lust, temptation, and sin.

- Your *body* is the temple of the Holy Spirit. It's where your spirit and soul dwell.
- Your *soul* is made up of your thoughts, emotions, and will. It comprises your human desires and passions. Its natural condition is selfishness and pride. It's the aggressive drive to please yourself. It's the part of you Paul called "the flesh" in his letters. Actually, Paul used the term in different ways, depending on the context. Sometimes he meant the physical body, but more often, he was referring to fallen human nature that is self-absorbed, self-promoting, and opposed to God's will and ways.
- Your *spirit* was dead but was made alive in Christ when you were saved. (See Eph. 2:1–7.) A person's spirit will live eternally—in heaven or hell. The body will be resurrected in the last judgment to be reunited with the spirit. A redeemed spirit is remade in the image of Christ. That's what it means to be "in Christ."

When we sin, we let our flesh rule over our spirits. As Paul explained, these two are always at war with each other—sometimes more obviously than others, but constantly. We can get discouraged because it sometimes looks as if we're losing. That's the nature of warfare, but it's not the whole story. God is always at work, in every aspect of our lives, to bring about His purposes. Paul ended his letter to the Christians in Thessalonica with this prayer: "May God himself, the God of peace, sanctify you through and through. May your whole spirit, soul and body be kept blameless at the coming of our Lord Jesus Christ. The one who calls you is faithful, and he will do it" (1 Thess. 5:23–24).

Paul didn't mince words when he talked about this fight, but he recognized the tension between the already and the not yet. To the Galatians, he wrote, "Those who belong to Christ Jesus *have crucified* the flesh with its passions and desires. Since we live by the Spirit, let us keep in step with the Spirit" (Gal. 5:24–25, italics added). But to the Romans and Ephesians, Paul wrote that our daily fight against sin involves *continually* crucifying the flesh, the sinful nature. (See Rom. 8:13 and Eph. 4:20–24.)

So, we were crucified with Christ when we became believers, but we still need to crucify our flesh when selfishness tries to run our lives. How can we do that?

We were crucified with Christ when we became believers, but we still need to crucify our flesh when selfishness tries to run our lives.

***Agree with what God says* about you.**

Pride, guilt, shame, fear, and doubt can plague us and cloud our minds. When we're under stress, we can forget what God has said is true of us. The Bible describes our identity in many wonderful ways: We have been chosen by God to be His dear children; we are inscribed on the palms of His hands; we are fearfully and wonderfully made; He will never leave us or forsake us, so we are secure in His love; God loves us as much as He loves Jesus; we are more valuable to Him than the stars in the sky.

When we trust in Jesus to forgive us and make us new people, we get a new identity, a new nature, and a new destiny. Even more, God injects His spiritual DNA into us. John described it this way: "No one who is born of God will continue to sin, because God's seed remains in them; they cannot go on sinning, because they have been born of God. This is how we know who the children of God are and who the children of the devil are: Anyone who does not do what is right is not God's child, nor is anyone who does not love their brother and sister" (1 John 3:9–10).

It's not that we can't sin, but that we can no longer be content with sin in our lives. It doesn't belong any more. Many unbelievers are extremely happy in their sinful ways, but no child of God is happy living in sin. The Spirit of God convicts us, makes us feel uncomfortable, ruins our sleep, and calls us to come back to the love, joy, and obedience of being a beloved son or daughter.

***Agree with what the Word of God says* about your life.**

The Bible doesn't give instructions about computers and cars, but it has brilliant insights about our purpose in life, God's nature, relationships, money, hope, joy, and growth—among countless other topics. Many people assume God doesn't have much to say to them, but those people haven't read the Bible! It has tons to say about the things that really matter.

Don't be passive; fight back!

If we're not convinced we're in a fight, we're going to get beaten up pretty badly. The battleground is mostly between our ears. Our thoughts are the proving ground for truth and the battleground against lies. In one of his letters to the Corinthians, Paul explained, "For though we live in the world, we do not wage war as the world does. The weapons we fight with are not the weapons of the world. On the contrary, they have divine power to demolish strongholds. We demolish arguments and every pretension that sets itself up against the knowledge of God, and we take captive every thought to make it obedient to Christ" (2 Cor. 10:3–5).

Our thoughts are the proving ground for truth and the battleground against lies.

Do you hear his military language? "War," "weapons," "fight," "divine power," "strongholds," "demolish," "captive." The warfare Paul describes isn't a Special Ops operation. It's a siege. We keep fighting and fighting and fighting, patiently pursuing the enemy within, and killing every trace of selfishness, deceit, pride, greed, and any other kind of fleshly desire we discover. And each time, we replace it with faith in God's unconditional love and gracious purposes for our lives.

Rest in the Father's embrace.

God isn't shocked when we struggle, but I'm sure He grieves when we turn our backs and walk away because we have given up on Him. In our darkest moments, we need to cling to the One whose love may seem a million miles away but is as close as our breath. The great saints of the Old Testament suffered and failed many times. What made them great wasn't an easy life with no struggles; it was their tenacity to get up and get going again when they fell.

You are God's child, and no one can steal your inheritance. The more time you spend with the Father, the more the Spirit will bear witness to your spirit that you belong to Him. Rest in His embrace—especially when you feel like running away.

When you feel frustrated, worried, enraged, impatient, afraid, or distraught, you may have lost your awareness of the embrace of the Father. When you forget about His love and His gracious purposes, you are walking in the flesh.

Ask the Father to bring your thoughts and emotions back into alignment with the Word of God.

How do you accomplish this? By praying in the Spirit. In Romans, Paul explained that when we can't pray, the Spirit prays for us with "groans too deep for words" (Rom. 8:26). He's interceding literally "in the Spirit." In his letter to the Corinthians, Paul explained that when you pray in tongues, you are praying in languages of men and angels (1 Cor. 13:1). The Spirit of God is praying through you back to the Father exactly what the Spirit knows you should pray (1 Cor. 14:2). When you pray in the Spirit, you build up your spiritual man (1 Cor. 14:4) because God is speaking through you back to himself, so it's always in accord with His will. That's why Paul says, "I wish all of you would pray in tongues" (1 Cor. 14:5).

One week at our church, I got on my knees to model what it looks like to pray and get in alignment with the Spirit of God—to bring your soul and flesh into submission to the Father. I prayed in the Spirit and in English just like Paul instructed (1 Cor. 14:13–14). After the service I felt a little concerned about it—concerned that someone might have been offended or confused by it . . . or perhaps scared because they didn't understand what it means to pray in the Spirit. As I considered it, the Spirit brought two things to mind:

- First, many of our people had never had "praying in the Spirit" modeled for them. Paul told the Ephesians to "pray in the Spirit on all occasions" (Eph. 6:18). When I was a boy, I would wake up in the morning and hear my dad praying in the Spirit. On the way to school, my mother sang in the Spirit. This experience was normal for me . . . and it's normal for people who are filled with the Spirit.

- Second, I needed to explain and emphasize the baptism in the Spirit. People may get offended, confused, or scared by the baptism in the Holy Spirit (or the spiritual experience of speaking in tongues) because they don't understand it. Also, the natural man doesn't like it at all. Why? Because the mind, intellect, will, and emotions are bypassed when we pray in the Spirit. We're used to thinking before we speak, but when we pray in the Spirit, our hearts pray without interference from our minds. It's completely normal for those who are unfamiliar with tongues to feel uncomfortable with it—and especially, for analytical people to resist it. Dr. Paul Brooks has noted that in his church, "The Spirit wants to raise both a voice *for God* (prophecy) and a voice *to God* (tongues/interpretation) through various inspired utterances as described in 1 Corinthians 12–14."[4]

The Enemy of our souls doesn't want the church of Jesus Christ to be freed, led, and empowered by the Spirit of

God. He will create confusion, so we need clarity. He brings division, so we need God's love and forgiveness. He sows deception, so we need truth. He injects doubt, so we need confidence in the goodness and greatness of God.

The Enemy doesn't want people to activate their prayer language because he knows it will strengthen them and make them more like Christ.

The Enemy doesn't want people to activate their prayer language because he knows it will strengthen them and make them more like Christ. Just imagine the problem he would have if everyone in your church was "praying in the Spirit on all occasions" (Eph. 6:18).

The Enemy is going to do anything and everything to keep people from receiving this capacity for powerful prayer. And if people speak in a prayer language, he will try to discredit them with pride. He will try to make them feel superior to "those people" who don't speak in tongues. Don't be deceived. Speaking in tongues doesn't make you superior to people or churches who don't. It just makes you superior to the person you were before you received the Spirit's power (Acts 1:8).

A Spirit-led life comes from a Spirit-filled life. Some people try to say that being filled with the Spirit makes life easy, "like being in the jet stream of God's power." This kind of experience happens sometimes, but like we saw in the passage in Isaiah, sometimes the Spirit enables us to fly, sometimes He gives us the strength to run, and sometimes we must depend on the depth of His love and power just to take one more step without fainting and falling. No, it's often not easy. In fact, it's a fight to stay intimately in touch with the Spirit of God, to walk hand in hand with the King of all, and to want His will more than anything on earth.

At the beginning of this chapter, I was honest about my struggles with jealousy, self-promotion, exaggeration, and other sins of the flesh. I had identified all of those (and more) many years before, but I never got victory over them until the new day dawned in my heart and at our church. I've had more clarity, more power, more joy, and more freedom than ever because the Spirit has been unleashed in my life. I have a friend who isn't shocked by my honesty. In fact, John and I have committed to complete honesty with each other. He has my back and I have his. When we pray together, it's never routine. We pray in the Spirit, and we sense God's powerful touch. For years, my goal was to manage my soul and limit the damage sin could do. Now we've created a culture of honesty, spiritual power, and freedom—in our friendship, in my family, and in our church. I still struggle with plenty of things, but now, I'm winning.

THINK ABOUT IT . . .

1. How would you describe the tension between the "already" and the "not yet"?

2. How does understanding and believing the four blessings in Romans 8 give us confidence to walk in the Spirit?

3. Read Romans 8:13–14. What are some ways the Holy Spirit leads you?

4. Which principle about "the fight" stands out to you? How can you apply it today?

CHAPTER 5

THE LOST AND THE LEAST

The Holy Spirit came at Pentecost—and continues today—to glorify Jesus Christ (John 16:14). His primary role is to shine a light on Jesus' love, power, purpose, and grace—to enlighten the eyes of our hearts so that we marvel at Jesus' humility in sacrificing His life for undeserving sinners. He provokes our wonder at His exaltation through the resurrection and ascension to the right hand of the Father where He reigns as King forever. As the Spirit glorifies Christ in us, our hearts gradually become tuned to His. We care about the things He cares about, we weep over the things that break His heart, and we are outraged over injustice just like He was.

What are those things? It's not a mystery. When Jesus returned from the desert where Satan tempted Him, He gave His first sermon. As the people watched in a synagogue in Nazareth, He opened the scroll of Isaiah and read a prophetic passage that was being fulfilled right before their eyes:

> "The Spirit of the Lord is on me,
> because he has anointed me
> to proclaim good news to the poor.
>
> He has sent me to proclaim freedom for the prisoners
> and recovery of sight for the blind,
> to set the oppressed free,
> to proclaim the year of the Lord's favor." (Luke 4:18–19)

For the next three years, His disciples, His enemies, and every person in every village where He traveled saw Jesus live out His purpose: to love the lost and the least, the sinners and the sick, the high and the low, the outcasts and the misfits. His Nazareth message was at the beginning of His ministry. At the end, He told His followers to make disciples and teach them "everything I have commanded you" (Matt. 28:20). What had He commanded them? To do the same things they had seen Him do every day they were with Him—to go anywhere people needed to hear the good news of the gospel and to shower love on every hurting person.

Others often misunderstood and condemned Jesus for loving those people, but He never wavered. It was His calling, and as we are filled with the Spirit and live Spirit-led lives, it's our calling too.

We need to consider the implications of Pentecost on our purpose and calling as Christians. In some churches, the filling of the Spirit may be more about shouting, dancing, and the expression of the sign gifts. We're not in competition to be more expressive and dramatic than other churches or individuals. When believers engage in a form of spiritual self-indulgence, lost people and hurting people may feel confused and awkward instead of informed and loved.

We can look at the problem from a different perspective. Some have observed that many people today aren't seeking the baptism in the Holy Spirit because they don't have a deep thirst for God, or they lack a desperate need for God to work in them and through them to have an impact on the lost and the least. When the disciples saw Jesus healing the sick, raising the dead, proclaiming the gospel, and praying to the Father, they realized they couldn't do any of those powerful acts on their own! They became sponges to soak up every bit of what Jesus could give them. The whole point of Spirit baptism isn't about us; it's about what God wants to do through us to have an impact on others. We must recapture the message of Acts 1:8. Jesus taught that when the Holy Spirit comes upon us, we will experience the power to be witnesses, not about ourselves, but about Him.

The whole point of Spirit baptism isn't about us; it's about what God wants to do through us to have an impact on others.

Some Christians are involved in evangelism and compassion ministries, but with mixed motives at best. They want to win people to Christ to prove themselves and receive applause. They're involved in helping people who are hurting, and they make sure others notice. Don't get me wrong. All of us have mixed motives to some degree. Our hearts won't be completely free from the taint of selfishness and sin on this side of heaven, but a sign of Spirit-filled, Spirit-led ministry is selfless, sacrificial love that is content to serve in secret where only the Father sees what we're doing. We are more content with His reward than the applause of people.

I know that pastors and other church leaders can work hard in ministry yet miss God's heart. I've been there. Years ago when our boys were little, Jenni and I often went to their soccer practices and games. Jenni stood on the sidelines talking to the other parents, but I took books and notes and sat by myself studying for the next week's sermon. One day, Jenni came over where I was sitting and asked, "Scott, what are you doing?"

I could tell it wasn't a casual question. I felt a bit threatened, so I snapped back, "What do you think I'm doing? I'm reading and studying for my sermon."

She looked into my eyes and said, "You're over here by yourself while twenty parents are within a few feet of you. If you would talk to them, you'd know almost all of them are struggling in their marriages, with their kids, in their careers, with their finances, or with health problems. These people need someone to care enough to connect with them and help them."

It was a surprising interruption, and I realized the "someone" she was talking about was me. But she wasn't finished. She asked, "Are you telling me—and them—that they don't count because they don't come to your church?" She turned around and walked back to the sidelines to hang out with the other parents.

I wanted to find some justification for my isolation, but there wasn't any. I realized I was going to talk to our church about Spirit-filled living, but I was out of tune with the heart of Jesus. I put my books and notes away, and I walked over to talk to the other parents. I never used soccer games or practice for sermon prep again. I began connecting with the lost and the least—even if they never set foot in The Oaks.

THE ELDER BROTHER

Jesus had a conversation with some religious leaders that was eerily similar to Jenni's words to me that day on the sidelines. Luke sets the scene for what is, perhaps, Jesus' most famous parable. One of the most remarkable things about Jesus was that the "worst" people of His society loved hanging out with Him, but the "best"

One of the most remarkable things about Jesus was that the "worst" people of His society loved hanging out with Him, but the "best" people despised Him.

people despised Him. Luke tells us, "Now the tax collectors and sinners were all gathering around to hear Jesus. But the Pharisees and the teachers of the law muttered, 'This man welcomes sinners and eats with them'" (Luke 15:1–2).

Take a good look at the groups that surrounded Jesus that day. *Tax collectors* weren't like our IRS officials. They collaborated with the Roman occupation force to collect imperial taxes from the Jewish people, and they often charged an excessive amount and pocketed the difference. They were considered traitors by almost everyone in the culture. *Sinners* were people who didn't follow the law of God, and they publicly flouted their sins. They were pimps, prostitutes, liars, self-absorbed manipulators, and rebels of every sort.

Though the *Pharisees* (and their cohorts, the teachers of the law) have gotten a bad reputation from those who read the Gospels, they were the good guys in Jewish society. They were dedicated to God and to the Scriptures. Under Roman occupation, they were models of consistency in temple worship, prayer, giving, and following the religious traditions. They felt threatened by the Romans, and they despised the tax collectors and sinners. They were suspicious of anyone who didn't toe their party line—anyone like Jesus.

And, of course, *Jesus' disciples* are another group in the scene. It was a tension-filled, pressure-packed moment—like opposing groups of defiant protesters meeting in the street. Jesus had them all exactly where He wanted them. He told them three stories that are really all part of the same lesson.

The first parable (Luke 15:3–7) was about a shepherd who lost a sheep. In this story, there was something lost (a sheep) and someone (a shepherd) who searched for what was lost. There was also a great celebration including the shepherd and all his friends when the lost sheep was found.

In the second story (Luke 15:8–10), a woman lost a coin. Once again, something was lost (a coin) and someone (the woman) looked for it. When she found it, she threw a party, which included the woman and her friends.

These celebrations produced the sound of heaven—the same kind of celebration the angels hold in heaven when a sinner comes to Christ. There was a clear pattern forming, but Jesus threw them a curve in the third story.

In the third story (Luke 15:11–32)—the famous parable of the prodigal son—there was not some*thing* that was lost, but some*one*—a son. A dad had two sons. The younger son asked his father for his share of the inheritance, which was like saying, "I wish you were dead!" His father gave it to him, and the son left home and "squandered his wealth in wild living" (Luke 15:13). Starving in a foreign land, the young man was desperate. He found a job feeding pigs, a role that would have shocked the Pharisees listening to Jesus tell this story. A Jewish person couldn't sink any lower than that!

One day in the pigpen, the young man had a revelation: he could go home and work for his father. He didn't expect to be reinstated as a son. It was too late for that, he was sure. But his father was kind and generous to his workers. Laboring for his dad would be a better life than feeding those pigs every day. He carefully prepared his confession and his request to become a hired hand on what was left of his father's estate.

As he approached his home, he was surprised by a strange sight: his father was running down the road toward him! When his dad came near, the returning son tried to blurt out his confession, but his dad didn't let him finish. He grabbed him, held him tight, and kissed him. Then he fully reinstated his son into the family with a robe, sandals, and a signet ring that was used to mark contracts.

Like the other two stories, the father threw a grand feast to celebrate the fact that his lost son had been found. But unlike the other stories, this wasn't the end. A servant told the older son about his brother's return and the feast his father was having for him. He was so angry that he refused to join the party. His father went out to ask him to come and celebrate, but he snarled his refusal.

This moment in the story wasn't lost on the people sitting and standing around Jesus. In that culture, it was the older brother's responsibility to go out to find his wayward sibling and bring him home. The tax gatherers and sinners were the younger brother in the story, and the Pharisees were the older brother. But the Pharisees hadn't gone out to seek and save the sinners and outcasts sitting at Jesus' feet. They were like the older brother in the story—angry, self-righteous, superior to "those people" . . . and immobile.

Jesus' point was that devotion is *all about* being close to the Father's heart, having the same heart the Father has for lost people, and sacrificing comfort and resources to search for them and bring them home.

The older brother was doing all kinds of hard work on the farm, and he was proud of it! He felt so superior to his brother that he couldn't even call him by name. He barked at his dad, "Look! All these years I've been slaving for you and never disobeyed your orders. Yet you never gave me even a young goat so I could celebrate with my friends. But when this son of yours who has squandered your property with prostitutes comes home, you kill the fattened calf for him" (Luke 15:29–30).

Devotion is *all about* being close to the Father's heart, having the same heart the Father has for lost people, and sacrificing comfort and resources to search for them and bring them home.

That was exactly the attitude the Pharisees had toward their sinful "younger brothers," and it was exactly their response to Jesus' love for sinners.

The older brother in Jesus' story—and the Pharisees and too many of us today—are extremely devoted, but to the wrong things. We're devoted to our reputations, to our prestige, and to our power instead of the Father's purposes. Like the older brother, we're working hard for Him, staying close to Him physically but very distant from His heart. The older brother was constantly around the father, but he wasn't captured by his father's love.

What a tragedy! When I think about the older brother in the story, it makes me incredibly sad. I imagine he woke up every day, thinking about himself, never recognizing how broken his father was over losing a son. He never noticed the way his dad sat on the porch, watching for any sign that his lost son was on his way back home. And I can imagine the grief in the dad's heart when he realized his older son didn't care enough about his brother to go look for him.

If the older brother or the Pharisees—or you and I—cared about the broken heart of our Father, we wouldn't just eat with Him, talk with Him, work for Him, and pray to Him. We would pray *with Him* for our lost brothers. And we would move heaven and earth in our search for them . . . until we found them.

I think Jesus wanted the people listening to Him that day—and us—to imagine what would have happened if the third story had worked out like the other two. They might have envisioned quite a different ending. After the young man left home, the older brother would have talked and prayed with his dad as they grieved about his brother's poor choices. Before long, he would have packed some traveling gear and headed out to look for him. He would have looked everywhere until he found his lost brother. The search may have taken months, but nothing would have stopped him.

His first glimpse may have been of his little brother eating scraps in the pigpen. He would have gotten down in the mud with him, hugged him, and begged him to come home. The younger brother would insist, "I'm not worthy to be called Dad's son anymore."

But the older brother would have assured him, "You've messed up horribly, but you're still Dad's son and you're still my brother."

The younger son wouldn't have walked home alone. Instead, the father would have been looking down the road at two brothers walking arm in arm. The older brother would have left his dad and brother hugging each other in the street while he ran in the house shouting, "My brother's home! My brother's home! Get everything ready for a feast tonight!" He would run to the closet where he knew his dad kept a clean robe and sandals all those months as he hoped and prayed for his younger son's return. He would have carried them to his dad so he could give them to his brother. The three of them would have stood in a circle in the middle of the street, arms around each other, crying, hugging, and rejoicing. And the feast would be the biggest party the community had ever seen!

But the scene I just described didn't happen. The Pharisees didn't love the tax collectors and sinners enough to pursue them, know them, eat with them, and love them. However, someone else loved them that much.

Jesus was the ultimate and true older brother. He did what the Pharisees should have done. He didn't just leave the comfort of a home in Palestine to look for and find sinners. He stepped out of unimaginable splendor of heaven to search and die for younger brothers—all of us. The old hymn puts it perfectly:

> He left His Father's throne above,
> So free, so infinite His grace;
> Emptied Himself of all but love,
> And bled for Adam's helpless race.[5]

When the Spirit shines His light on the marvelous grace of Jesus, He melts our hearts and remolds them to become more like His. Devotion to our careers makes us more like the older brother, but devotion to the Father transforms us and gives us genuine compassion for the lost and the least.

When the Spirit shines His light on the marvelous grace of Jesus, He melts our hearts and remolds them to become more like His.

Is there someone in your life who needs your unconditional love and acceptance? Is the Spirit prompting you to call or reach out in love to someone? If your Spirit-filled living doesn't drive you to the pigpens of this world looking for your lost brothers and sisters, you're missing the whole point of Spirit baptism—and you're missing the heart of the Father. If you think Christianity is only about doing what God wants so you can get what you want, then maybe you and your Father need to have a talk . . . like the talk the dad in the story had with his older son.

God is inviting us to come to the feast, and, even more, He's expecting us to care enough about misfits and outcasts to find them and bring them home—and that's what a baptism of power motivates and equips us to do.

THE TALK

I believe God wants to have this talk with many of us. But first, we need to understand why the older brother was so angry. He felt cheated. He felt overlooked. He felt a ton of self-pity and pride and arrogance. He started his response to his dad's invitation with an insult. He said, "Look!" I can imagine him jabbing his finger toward his dad as he said it. This was the greatest day of his father's life—his lost son had come home! But the older son was furious that his dad had showered his brother with affection and acceptance. He said, "I've been a slave for you!" It's ironic, isn't it? The repentant younger son offered to be his father's servant, but the resistant older son thought of himself as a slave . . . and resented every minute . . . even though his father treated him like a prince! He was saying, "Hey, look! I'm the faithful one. I've done everything right! Haven't you even noticed?" Some of us feel the same way when we see God shower blessings on people who haven't worked as hard or as long as we have. We want to shout, "It's not fair!" Indeed, it's not. It's grace, and we could have been bathing in it all along in the Father's presence, but we were too driven to prove ourselves to notice His kindness, tenderness, and gentleness.

I've talked to pastors who resented news that God was blessing other churches. I've been one of those pastors! But the disease of "older brother-itis" isn't limited to the pulpit. There are plenty of Pharisee badges to go around in our churches! We need to hear what the dad told his son as they stood in the field that day.

"You are always with me."

The Father says to us that He's always with us, in good and bad times, no matter what. Why are we so driven? Because we're still insecure. As we experience the unbounded love of the Father, we can relax, unwind, and enjoy knowing and loving Him in return. And we'll stop comparing our lives, our finances, and our ministries with anyone else. We'll be wonderfully content to know that we belong to Him, and He's all we need. The focus of sonship shouldn't be "what can I get from my Father," but "how can I get closer to my

Father, how can I become more like Him, how can I please Him, and how can I make His heart sing?"

"Everything I have is yours."

The father in Jesus' story made everything crystal clear to his older son: "Your inheritance is not in jeopardy because your brother came home. Everything I have is yours, so don't get mad because I bless your brother. That doesn't take anything away from what I have for you." Our Father says the same to us: Stop comparing yourself to others; stop keeping score. ("He got a fattened calf, but I haven't even gotten a goat!") No one can steal your inheritance in Christ. Relax. Enjoy the Father's love. You don't have to make anything happen. You don't have to press, strive, and shove your way into getting what's yours. Your inheritance is safe in the Father's hands.

"Please celebrate your brother's return with me."

The dad in the story pleaded with his older son to join the celebration. His younger son's return was an answer to prayer, the greatest joy he could imagine! And he wanted his other son to celebrate just as much. In the first two stories, a party was held for the one who searched and the neighbors. In the third story, no one went out to search, and the one who should have gone didn't want to celebrate—even when his gracious dad came out to plead with him to come in. When we hear about God's blessings in the lives of other leaders, the Father is saying to you and me, "Please stop thinking about yourself and realize that the lost need to be found and brought back home. They were dead, but now they're home safe. My heart isn't broken anymore. I'm thrilled! Please rejoice with me!"

BRINGING IT HOME

When we read the end of the story, we see something touching and heart-wrenching. The father was tender with his furious and resistant older son. He addressed him, "My son." The Greek word used there is very affectionate. It could read "my child." The father didn't yell at his son, and he didn't blame him for not going out to find his brother. He was gentle and kind in his invitation. Remember, the older brother represented the Pharisees. Jesus was saying to these fierce, harsh, condemning, judgmental people, "My child, don't be so angry. I love these people, and if you really knew the Father's love, you would love them too." But they didn't get the message. Only weeks later, they hatched their plot to kill Him.

Is the Spirit of the Lord on you? He has anointed you to preach good news to the poor, to proclaim freedom to those who are spiritually or actually in prison, to heal the sick and restore sight to the blind, to release the oppressed, and to proclaim God's favor to everyone who will listen.

We say we follow Christ, but do we? We need to look at our circle of inclusion. Who is outside our circle? Who is excluded? We may not label those people as "unworthy," but ignoring them brings the same results. Do we share the gospel and care for the needs of only those who appreciate our efforts? Jesus didn't have this restriction. Do we reach out only to those who look like us? Jesus loved even the hated Samaritans . . . and the Pharisees, too! Do we avoid smelly people, awkward people, loud people, or quiet people? Do we steer clear of those who can't contribute anything to our success? Jesus poured His life and His blood out for the undeserving—people like you and me.

When I find a cigarette butt in our parking lot, or I see a six-pack in the back seat of a car, or I hear that a gay or lesbian couple is in our service, I'm not outraged. I don't try to bar the doors to keep those people out. I'm thrilled! It shows that we're becoming the kind of church that is captured by the heart of Jesus. He was a friend of sinners. They felt His love, and they wanted to be with Him. I want our church to be known as a place that welcomes sinners, too. We have some Pharisees in our church. Every congregation has its share. But gradually, God is changing the culture of our church. The fullness of the Spirit compels us to love the lost and the least just as Jesus did. It drives us out of our comfort zones and into the pigpens where we'll find our lost brothers and sisters and beg them to come home. It's a beautiful thing to see.

THINK ABOUT IT . . .

1. What are some reasons it's so easy to rationalize or excuse being a "Pharisee" today?

2. What does it mean to "follow Christ" and have "the Spirit of the Lord on us" regarding the lost and the least?

3. How would you define and describe your circle of inclusion and exclusion? How would Jesus describe your circle?

SECTION 3

GAME CHANGER

(SCOTT'S VOICE)

CHAPTER 6

RULES OF ENGAGEMENT

Let me go back to the day when I announced there was "a new day" at our church. The services were exhilarating! I was so excited about what the Spirit of God had done among us. I had given God "one minute" of the service, and He had given back far, far more. On the drive home after the service, my excitement suddenly turned to anxiety. I thought, *Oh, no. What now? What's next? What have I gotten myself into? Have I just opened the floodgates for craziness at our church?*

I wanted the "new day" to continue, but I was afraid of all the strange things that can happen if people misuse the gifts. I called John to ask for help because he was way ahead of me in knowing how to make all this come together. We met on Tuesday so he would have time to download the principles and practices of how they did it at Freedom Fellowship International. John's church was a decade ahead of us in knowing how to steward the public gifts in a contemporary church without getting weird. I listened to everything that John had to say, and together we wrote out a spiritual gifts "user manual" for The Oaks. After I had it organized, I sent it to a couple of men I respect who are Bible college professors. They gave me some good ideas and feedback.

At that point I felt comfortable with where we were going, but I had another important step to take. On Wednesday night I met with our elders to share the "participation process" so every believer could be involved in the movement of the Spirit in our services. That step was crucial. I was committed to a unified leadership—on this issue and every other important issue facing the church. Thankfully, they were excited about the direction I sensed God was taking us. I made sure they all understood the biblical foundation, the principles, and the practices we were going to roll out at The Oaks. I would have taken more time to answer their questions if they had been hesitant. We needed to be on the same page so we could support each other every step of the way. My role as a leader is to inform, encourage, and provide direction. In fact, my main role is to help our leaders experience the presence and the power of God so all of us flow in the Spirit. If you want to enlist people to participate in a Spirit-led movement, you can't do it alone. You have to engage church leaders in a prayerful process before public announcements are made.

Our "rules of engagement" weren't written to restrict the Holy Spirit, but to provide clarity and direction for every person in our church to use the Spirit's gifts in a God-honoring, powerful way. If people understood the process, they wouldn't feel awkward or uncomfortable when the gifts were exercised.

God encouraged me that this wasn't going to be a movement of His Spirit centered around pastors or a few people flowing in the gifts like they had a corner on the spirituality market. It was to be a marketplace movement for everybody—as Paul wrote: varieties of gifts, varieties of ministries, varieties of effects (1 Cor. 12:4–6). According to Paul, when the members of the body of Christ come together, each one has something crucial to offer (1 Cor. 12:27). Yes, I'm on stage almost every Sunday, but I'm the Equipper-in-Chief and the Lead Follower. As the pastor, I am called to teach and instruct others how to flow with the leading of the Spirit. My role is to prepare them and provide a fireplace for God to send the Spirit's fire.

During the week, and increasingly as Sunday approached, I felt an odd blend of excitement and dread. I was thrilled with what the Spirit of God had done the previous Sunday, and I wanted to see what He would do again and again. But I had flashbacks of weird things that happened in church when I was a boy, and I desperately wanted to avoid such things! I was opening a door, and I wasn't sure who or what was going to walk through it. If that happened, our "new day" would become "doomsday." Instead of having 2,500 excited, expectant, responsive people, I'd have someone dancing in the aisles with about a hundred people in the remnant who were left of The Oaks. Yeah, I was scared.

As you probably guessed, it all worked out. The Spirit has shown up every week. The new day continues. In our study, prayer, and conversations, we developed practices for prophecy, tongues, and interpretation in our worship services. These are accessible (and adaptable) to every church looking for a "new day."

In our study, prayer, and conversations, we developed practices for prophecy, tongues, and interpretation in our worship services.

I believe Paul's message to the Corinthian church about their use of gifts was instructive but not exhaustive. His main point was that gifts should be used in a decent and orderly manner, but there's some flexibility in how a church can implement an orderly expression of the gifts in a worship service. Our process reflects this flexibility. Everything we do, and the guidelines we use, are in alignment with Paul's intentions.

REGARDING PROPHECY

In his letter to the Corinthians to clarify the purpose and public expression of spiritual gifts, Paul explained, "But he who prophesies speaks edification and exhortation and comfort to men" (1 Cor. 14:3, NKJV). God's intention for all prophecy is to build up, to exhort people to follow Him, and to comfort those who are hurting (see also 1 Cor. 14:24–25).

God can give a prophetic word through any believer for the purpose of encouraging and teaching His people (1 Cor. 14:31). Sometimes I'm prompted to say, "I sense that God wants to speak to us right now in a special way. Let's take a moment to listen for His voice." In such times, the Spirit may prompt a prophetic word to be given by someone in the body (1 Cor. 14:29–33; 1 Thess. 5:12).

We may think of the Old Testament prophets standing against the people, looking fierce, and pronouncing judgment on them. This isn't the New Testament prophetic model that we see in Christ or one that lines up with the instructions given by Paul in 1 Corinthians 14:3. All prophecy is for the encouragement, strengthening, and comfort of others. We are called to follow the ministry pattern of Jesus. He was blunt in calling people to repent, but He was tender and gentle with sinners. They knew He loved them—even when they were sinning! Our prophetic words need to be bathed in the same kind of love, forgiveness, and acceptance. God isn't furious. He may be disappointed and grieved, but He isn't harsh. The words we receive or give from Him should have the spirit (and the Spirit) of Jesus. It is, Paul told us, the kindness of God that leads to repentance (Rom. 2:4). Let all prophecy be spoken from a heart of kindness and love. The public gift of tongues is given as a sign to unbelievers so they will be convinced and convicted that God is really speaking to them.

REGARDING TONGUES AND INTERPRETATION

These gifts are for the edification of the church, not to build a person's reputation (1 Cor. 14:5, 12). The public manifestation of tongues is a prayer, praise, or thanksgiving to God, yet it functions as a supernatural sign—a sign to convict unbelievers that God is really present in their midst.

The public gift of tongues and the interpretation of tongues is not the same as prophecy. Prophecy is for believers (and unbelievers), but the public expression of tongues is primarily used as a sign (an alarm) to get the unbeliever's attention. As my friend John says, "God uses it as a 'supernatural altar call'" (1 Cor. 14:22–25). There shouldn't be more than three public expressions of tongues and interpretations (divine altar calls) in one meeting (1 Cor. 14:27).

If an expression of tongues commands the attention of the corporate gathering, there must always be an interpretation so the people in the service can benefit from it (1 Cor. 14:27–28). In this way Paul indicates that Spirit-inspired prayers, blessings, and thanksgivings may be understood and owned by those in attendance (1 Cor. 14:16–17). These activities function as a sign to the unbelievers that God is commanding their attention, inviting them to look for Him, know Him, love Him, and follow Him.

These biblical instructions don't hinder the moving of the Spirit. In fact, they give God's people clear direction and a safe way to engage the gifts. After all, our worship gatherings should be a laboratory for believers to learn how to flow in the gifts so they can be more confident when the Spirit prompts them to use the gifts in the marketplace. That's one of the reasons why we tell people they don't need to give a prophecy or interpretation of tongues in King James English. God can speak Old English if He chooses, but He can speak in our modern day vernacular as well. We will be more fruitful in the marketplace if we are more "naturally supernatural" in our voice, tone, and vocabulary.

WEEK TWO AND BEYOND

The next Sunday morning, I placed elders across the front of each section at the end of the rows. I shared with everyone what the Scripture says: We can all prophesy, we are expecting God to speak through all of us, and we should all be hearing from God. I instructed them:

> If you have a word from the Lord during worship, write it down and bring it up to one of the elders in the front. They will read it and judge whether it is for the service right then, for a later time, or for some other purpose. Don't be offended if it isn't used immediately. It's not your word. You're just the postman. Give it—that's all God expects from you. Let the elders judge how it should be used in ministry to the church.

I also explained that there will be times in the service when God will want us to be quiet and allow for a public expression of tongues and interpretation of tongues or a prophetic word. I said:

> Let me give you instructions about how this will work in our services. The Lord will impress on us that He wants to speak, so either I or the person who is leading the service will stop and say, "I sense God wants to speak to us right now. Let's pause and listen." One of three responses may happen: an expression of tongues and an interpretation (which is a divine altar call), or a prophetic word, or we will stand still in the presence of God and let Him speak to each of us as we listen for His voice. We ask that only those who are members in good standing here at The Oaks give a public word. If you aren't a member of The Oaks, we invite you to participate by writing out the prophetic word and bringing it to the elders up front—of course, not during the message, but during the singing or at the end of the service. That way we can make sure all can participate and everything is done in a decent and orderly way according to 1 Corinthians 14:40. And know this: God doesn't speak in King James English or in harsh tones. He speaks to us like we speak to a friend.

After we began this process, I was sitting in the front one Sunday morning during the worship songs, and God said to me, "I want to speak."

I replied, "Okay, I'll pause the service."

God said, "Brooks has the word."

One row over I saw Paul Brooks, one of the elders of our church. I turned to ask him if he had the prophetic word. As I walked toward him, his wife, Patricia, began telling him something. I asked Paul, "Do you have a word?"

He responded, "No, but Patricia does." They went to the front, and Patricia gave a powerful word from the Lord. It was the first time God had ever used her in this way. She spoke with such tenderness and brokenness that people began to weep throughout the church. Patricia is a very gentle person. She isn't one to take over a room full of people. She's gracious and deferential, and her message combined those traits with clarity and power. It was obvious that God was speaking through her. I love how God works!

THE HANDOUT

Let me be practical. I didn't want anyone going home and wondering, "What did Pastor Scott say about the gifts? What am I supposed to do . . . and not do?" To make sure our teaching was clear and our practice biblical, John and I wrote a handout for our church. Feel free to use it or adapt it to fit your leadership and your situation.[6]

PROPHECY IN PUBLIC WORSHIP

1 CORINTHIANS 14:3 (NKJV)

"But he who prophesies speaks edification and exhortation and comfort to men."

1 CORINTHIANS 14:24–25 (NKJV)

"But if all prophesy, and an unbeliever or an uninformed person comes in, he is convinced by all, he is convicted by all. And thus the secrets of his heart are revealed; and so, falling down on his face, he will worship God and report that God is truly among you."

1 CORINTHIANS 14:29–33 (NKJV)

"Let two or three prophets speak, and let the others judge. But if anything is revealed to another who sits by, let the first keep silent. For you can all prophesy one by one, that all may learn and all may be encouraged. And the spirits of the prophets are subject to the prophets. For God is not the author of confusion but of peace, as in all the churches of the saints."

All prophecy must be for edification, exhortation, and comfort (vv. 3, 24–25).

God can give a prophetic word through any believer for the purpose of encouraging and teaching His people (v. 31).

Instruction for The Oaks: If God gives you a word for the church during the service, write it out, bring it to the elders on the front row who will judge whether it is for now or later. You are the postman. It's God's word, not yours, so don't get offended by how or when it's used (v. 29).

"The spirit of the prophet is subject to the prophet." For those who say they "can't hold it," yes, you can (vv. 32–33).

There will come times when the pastor will say, "I sense that God wants to speak to us right now in a special way. Let's take a moment to listen for His voice." In these moments, a prophetic word can be given to the body by someone who is a member of The Oaks without writing it out, if the Spirit prompts someone to do so (v. 29).

TONGUES AND INTERPRETATION OF TONGUES IN PUBLIC WORSHIP

1 CORINTHIANS 14:5, 12 (NKJV)

"I wish you all spoke with tongues, but even more that you prophesied; for he who prophesies is greater than he who speaks with tongues, unless indeed he interprets, that the church may receive edification. . . . Even so you, since you are zealous for spiritual gifts, let it be for the edification of the church that you seek to excel."

Everything is to be done for the edification of the church (v. 5).

Don't be zealous about being used in the gifts so you can look important (v. 12).

1 CORINTHIANS 14:22–25 (NKJV)

"Therefore tongues are for a sign, not to those who believe but to unbelievers; but prophesying is not for unbelievers but for those who believe. Therefore if the whole church comes together in one place, and all speak with tongues, and there come in those who are uninformed or unbelievers, will they not say that you are out of your mind? But if all prophesy, and an unbeliever or an uninformed person comes in, he is convinced by all, he is convicted by all. And thus the secrets of his heart are revealed; and so, falling down on his face, he will worship God and report that God is truly among you."

The public expression of tongues is given as a sign to unbelievers so they will be convinced and convicted that the supernatural God is present, and it's important to respond to Him and His Word.

Tongues and interpretation is *not* the same as prophecy. Prophecy is for believers (and unbelievers). The public expression of tongues is primarily used as a sign (an alarm) to get the unbelievers' attention so God can speak to their hearts and call them to salvation. It is a supernatural altar call (vv. 22–25).

1 CORINTHIANS 14:27–28 (NKJV)

"If anyone speaks in a tongue, let there be two or at the most three, each in turn, and let one interpret. But if there is no interpreter, let him keep silent in church, and let him speak to himself and to God."

There shouldn't be more than three public expressions of tongues and interpretations (altar calls) in one meeting (vs. 27).

1 CORINTHIANS 14:39–40 (NKJV)

"Therefore, brethren, desire earnestly to prophesy, and do not forbid to speak with tongues. Let all things be done decently and in order."

The bottom line:

- Everyone should desire *earnestly* to prophesy (and for all the gifts).
- We shouldn't *forbid* speaking in tongues.
- Everything should be done decently and in *order*.

IMPORTANT NOTE:

There is no need for a prophecy or interpretation to be in King James English. God talks to us in our modern day vernacular. You don't need to speak with anger or in a different voice when God speaks through you. This should all be "naturally supernatural."

A NEW THING

It's the most exciting thing in the world to know that hundreds of people, the core of our spiritual movement, come to church excited because they can't wait to see what the Spirit of God is going to do among them. Over and over, I hear people say as they walk in, "Pastor Scott, I can't wait to hear what God is going to say to us today . . . and He might say it through me!" They know they have an opportunity. If God speaks to them, they might stand up and give a word, a tongue, or an interpretation, or they may write it on a card and give it to one of our elders. They may be prompted by the Spirit to minister to their family members as they're walking in or to pray for a guest in the concourse. Regardless of how it happens, they know that if God speaks to them, it matters. It matters a lot.

These people come to church thinking, *God may use me today. I can't wait to see what happens!* When church operates like this, we don't need to be afraid of the Holy Spirit any more. We can walk in awe of His wonders.

We still plan our services, but we always leave time for the Spirit to say and do whatever He wants to say and do. Everything we do is bathed in prayer. It's not that the planned part is fleshly and the open part is spiritual. It's all about God, for God, and from God, but we want to be sure we leave plenty of room for the Spirit to work apart from the service schedule. We plan the service, but we prepare our hearts for anything He wants to do.

God wants to do something new in you and in your church. He's asking you if you want it. All you have to do is open your heart to His leading. God often wants us to "turn the page" and experience the freshness of His Spirit. Through Isaiah, He told the people, "Forget the former things; do not dwell on the past. See, I am doing a new thing" (Isa. 43:18–19). The writer to the Hebrews reminds us, "The former regulation is set aside because it was weak and useless (for the law made nothing perfect), and a better hope is introduced, by which we draw near to God" (Heb. 7:18–19). The coming of Jesus broke a spiritual drought of over four hundred years, and the Holy Spirit's presence at Pentecost brought fresh wind and fresh fire to the people who trusted in Jesus—and to those who would trust Him because of the testimony of the 120 believers.

Are you ready for the sound of heaven to resound in your church? Stop trying to meticulously plan your life, your ministry, and your future, and then asking God to bless your plans. Instead, come to Him and seek His face. Be open to the movement of His Spirit. His will is better, His leading is better, and His way is already blessed. Long ago, God spoke words that are still true today:

> "If my people, who are called by my name, will humble themselves and pray and seek my face and turn from their wicked ways, then I will hear from heaven, and I will forgive their sin and will heal their land.

> Now my eyes will be open and my ears attentive to the prayers offered in this place. I have chosen and consecrated this temple so that my Name may be there forever. My eyes and my heart will always be there." (2 Chron. 7:14–16)

God wants us to seek His face far more than His blessing—to seek the Giver more than the gifts. When we sense His heart, our hearts will be filled to overflowing with His greatness and grace. We'll be all His, and we'll be all in.

If this is what you want, join me in this prayer:

> Lord, I humble myself before You. You are the great King and gracious Savior. I need You to fill me. I can't do Your work without Your Spirit guiding, empowering, and loving people through me. I want Your way, not mine. I want to experience Your heart in a fresh way. Only then will others sense Your love as I speak to them, care for them, and serve them. I need the fresh wind of Your Spirit to blow me in the direction You want me to go, and I need the fresh fire of Your Spirit to fuel everything I do. I'm Yours, Lord. I'm Yours.

Will you say yes to God's prompting? Will you be open to a new day in your own life and in your church? Don't wait until you feel completely comfortable and every question is answered. That day will never come. You'll be waiting until the end of time. Step out with what you know, on what you sense God is leading you to be and do. If you don't sense His leading, by all means, don't take a step! But if you do, find the courage to take His hand and start the adventure. Everyone's waiting for you. Your family, your leaders, your church, and your community are looking to you for a word from the Lord. Receive it, soak in it, and then give it to everyone you know.

It's a new day. Are you in?

THINK ABOUT IT . . .

1. Do the guidelines and processes in this chapter give you confidence and peace, or do they seem too constraining? Explain your answer.

2. How would your leaders respond to the handout and an explanation of the principles and practices?

3. Which aspects of the Rules of Engagement intrigue you? Which parts threaten you?

4. What's your next step?

CHAPTER 7

FROM THE PULPIT

As lunch began with some pastors in our area, one of them asked, "Hey Scott, what's going on at your church these days?"

I replied, "It's been amazing, really. Deep . . . life changing . . . powerful. God has been moving in an incredible way." I stopped for a second and then said, "And it's all happening because of me."

They all started laughing. They knew I had better social skills and spiritual awareness than to claim I was the source of all the great things happening in the church. One of them spoke for the rest with a smile and a hint of sarcasm, "Wow! It's all happening because of you, huh?" It was an invitation to explain myself.

I shook my head and told them, "I didn't mean it to come out like that. But in a way, it's true. A lot has been happening because God has been rebuking me so much and opening my eyes to blind spots in my life. It's been incredibly hard. Before God and our people, I have confessed and repented.

I realized I had been the cork in the bottle preventing the flow of God's Spirit. I had been the ceiling blocking how high God wanted to take our church. This situation had to change, and change comes hard . . . at least for me." They asked me to explain what had happened.

We had just experienced the largest attendance on an Easter weekend, with over 200 decisions for Christ. A few days later, I went to our weekly prayer meeting, but I felt dead . . . as if God had lifted His hand off my life. I assumed I was exhausted from all the preparations and services for Easter, but I could tell something wasn't right. Actually, the sense of God's absence scared me. I called John and asked him if I could meet him at his office so he and his prayer team could pray for me.

Just a few minutes after we started praying, God began giving them insight about why I was feeling like this. One of the men had a vision like a weather map with a storm moving over our church. He said, "God wants to pour out showers of His Spirit on The Oaks. But if you aren't in step with Him, you'll miss it. You're feeling anxious. You're starting to miss the Spirit."

Another one asked, "What are you hearing God say to you about the next few months at The Oaks? What is the trajectory of where He is taking you?"

I answered, "We are about to do a series called 'In Search of Oz.'" He asked me to tell him more about the series. I explained that Oz is about searching for things you need and want, but not depending on God.

He asked me where I got the idea for the series, and I told him it came from a pastor in Florida who is a friend of mine. He frowned and looked me in the eye: "That's not where you need to get direction. You're never going to see the results God wants The Oaks to have unless you get every word, every idea from the Lord."

Another friend said, "Scott, you're trying to be the Wizard. You're assuming you can give a heart to a Tin Man, a brain to a Scarecrow, and courage to a Cowardly Lion, but you can't. God has to do the work in people. Have you forgotten that?"

No, I hadn't forgotten. I understood what they were saying, and I didn't disagree. I just stood there confused, wondering how I got to this point. I asked God to show me what to do. On the way home I remembered that I needed to have a talk with my son Dakota about partial obedience—something had happened earlier in the morning, and it needed to be addressed. God gave me an idea. I told Dakota to read 1 Samuel 15 and write a one-page paper about it. About thirty minutes later, he came downstairs with his paper on the partial obedience of King Saul and how God took the kingdom of Israel away from him because He couldn't trust him. He had gotten the message about the dangers of doing only part of what God commands: Your sacrifices and offerings are only valuable to God when they are from a heart that is totally surrendered to Him—hearts that love Him, trust Him, and obey Him completely.

A WORD FOR THE MESSENGER

About an hour later, I dropped Dakota off at the church for drama practice. As soon as I was alone in the car, God said to me, "Son, when you get home, I want you to go to your room and write a paper for me on Revelation 3, the church at Laodicea. Tell me how the passage fits with what I'm saying to you right now."

When I got home I went back to my room and shut the door. I said, "God, speak to me. I want to know what You are saying." I opened my Bible and started reading the passage:

> To the angel of the church in Laodicea write: These are the words of the Amen, the faithful and true witness, the ruler of God's creation. I know your deeds, that you are neither cold nor hot. I wish you were either one or the other! So, because you are lukewarm—neither hot nor cold—I am about to spit you out of my mouth. You say, "I am rich; I have acquired wealth and do not need a thing." But you do not realize that you are wretched, pitiful, poor, blind and naked. I counsel you to buy from me gold refined in the fire, so you can become rich; and white clothes to wear, so you can cover your shameful nakedness; and salve to put on your eyes, so you can see.

> Those whom I love I rebuke and discipline. So be earnest and repent. Here I am! I stand at the door and knock. If anyone hears my voice and opens the door, I will come in and eat with that person, and they with me.
>
> To the one who is victorious, I will give the right to sit with me on my throne, just as I was victorious and sat down with my Father on his throne. Whoever has ears, let them hear what the Spirit says to the churches. (Rev. 3:14–22)

After slowly and carefully reading the passage, I wrote a number of things God showed me:

- The "angel" of the church is the messenger, or the preacher. Change has to start with me. God wants me to be a faithful witness. He sees into the recesses of my heart, whether I'm hot or cold. He knows that I'm wretched, pitiful, poor, blind, and naked.
- God graciously comes to me with gold refined in the fire—gold that's in the process of continual purification. It takes time, heat, and precision. I'm not going

> I'm not going to receive the true riches of God by holding on to the things of this world. I'll only get them from Him.

to receive the true riches of God by holding on to the things of this world. I'll only get them from Him.

- God wants to give me white clothes to cover my shame and my nakedness—clothes He has made specifically for me, a tailor-made ministry designed for The Oaks family and me. Also, He will give eye salve so I can see clearly the things of the Spirit—the things God wants to show our church.
- God disciplines and rebukes me because He loves me. He's my Father who loves me, in the same way I love Dakota and want him to learn and grow and become the man God wants him to be. I love my son so much. I want him to listen to me and open his heart fully to the truth he needs to hear. God told me, "That's how I feel about you! Please don't be stubborn. Listen to what I'm saying to you. Get serious about it and repent. This is a big deal. If you're going to become the person I want you to be, you have to trust Me at a whole new level. Everything you need is in Me—nowhere else."
- Jesus says, "I'm here at the door. I'm knocking. Open your heart and let Me in. I want to talk to you. Take the time to sit down and eat with Me. I'll tell you everything you need to know, and I'll feed you food with all the nutrients that you need. Then you'll be able to take that word and that food and give it to My people. Trust Me. I know what they need more than you do. Give them

what I give you—nothing more and nothing less—and then you'll see true repentance, change, freedom, and lasting fruit."

- Jesus is saying to me, "If you do this, I'll reward you. I'll give you a place near Me. I'll give you victory. You'll lead My people into a new freedom and victory like they've never experienced before. Trust Me, son. Trust Me."

I felt confused and ashamed. I asked the Lord, "How did this happen? How did I mess up this bad? Have I sinned? Are you telling me to confess sin to the people on Sunday?"

He said to me, "If you do the Oz series like you were planning to do, it's just because you sent out 55,000 invitations to the community, and you've invested time and money to build a set for the production. Yes, if you keep going in that direction, it's sin—because now you know I'm telling you to do something different."

God's word was crystal clear. The stage set for the series had already been completed, and I simply planned to tear it down. Before demolition began, I asked God, "So what do You want me to do?" He told me to keep the set up, and then dismantle it each week, little by little, until the stage was totally clear except for the cross.

The Lord told me to confess each week what I had planned to do, and then tell our congregation what God told me to do. They (and I) would see the massive difference between my ideas and His. Each week we took time during the service to tear down part of the Oz set on the stage and carry it off. Each week, we "cleared the stage" of anything that wasn't God's idea. We didn't need it. It was a distraction, and if we continued with the series according to my ideas, the props would be an idol, something we were trying to do to help God out instead of trusting that His instructions were enough.

A LOT LIKE PETER

I prayed and asked, "Lord, am I acting like Saul in 1 Samuel 15? Is this the sin of rebellion? Is this like the church in Laodicea? Are you going to spit me out of Your mouth?"

The Lord graciously replied, "No, Scott, you're more like Peter than Saul."

I guess that's encouraging. He reminded me that Peter was always trying to help Jesus. He thought he had to correct Jesus' plans and adjust His agenda. Remember, Jesus told Peter that He had to go to the cross and suffer at the hands of the religious leaders. That didn't fit into Peter's plans for the future—for Jesus or for His followers. Peter tried to correct Him, "No, Lord. Not that!"

Jesus gave His own correction: "Get behind Me, Satan. You aren't thinking with the thoughts of God, but with your own. Quit trying to help Me, because it isn't helping (Matt. 16:23, author's paraphrase)!"

Even at the Last Supper when Jesus tried to wash Peter's feet, Peter drew back and insisted, "No, you shall never wash my feet."

But Jesus told him, "Unless I wash you, you have no part with me."

It seemed Peter got the picture. He probably shouted, "Then, Lord, not just my feet but my hands and my head as well" (John 13:6–9). When I thought of this story, the Lord rebuked me, "Scott, quit trying to manage what I'm doing. Don't take away from it or try to add to it . . . just do what I say!"

In this conversation with Peter, Jesus predicted that His outspoken, confident follower would fail Him three times in the coming hours. But once again, Peter thought he knew more than Jesus. He insisted, "There's no way! I'll never deny you." But he was wrong. After Peter's third denial, the cock crowed. At that instant Jesus looked directly at Peter, and the fisherman "went outside and wept bitterly" (Luke 22:61–62).

Until Pentecost, Peter couldn't listen to Jesus and receive what He said. Peter had to be in control, to be in charge of Jesus' agenda, and it didn't work out very well for him! But Jesus didn't give up on him. After Jesus' crucifixion, Peter and some others were fishing, and in the early morning light they saw Jesus standing on the shore. Peter jumped in and swam to Him! In a tender and powerful restoration over a fish breakfast, Jesus asked Peter three times, "Do you love me?" The questions pierced Peter's heart. Three times he had denied even knowing Jesus, and now He asked three times for a recommitment of love and loyalty. Peter humbled himself and repented, and he was restored.

Jesus gave Peter a crucial role in the church: "to feed His sheep." Peter became the leader of the early church. In effect, Jesus was saying to him, "Trust Me that I know what My sheep need. Feed them what I give you to feed them. Quit trying to help Me. Quit adding your ideas to Mine. I'm calling you to a new level of love and trust. You will speak My words—nothing more and nothing less." (See John 21:1–21.)

That was God's message to me, too.

To our people at The Oaks, I confessed that I'm not the Wizard of Oz. I don't have anything to give them that will heal their hearts, provide wisdom for their lives, instill courage to face heartaches, heal their families, put strained marriages back together, or set them free. Only God can do that.

On the stage that day, I "pulled the curtain back" and told them that I will follow Christ with all my heart, and I will encourage them to follow Him, too.

The Lord told me that if we get this right—if I repent like Peter, He will bring the outpouring He wants to bring and do what He did in Acts 2 through Peter's preaching and leadership. The man portrayed in the early chapters of Acts is a very different person than the one we saw in the Gospels. Peter became humble, submissive, and pliable in the hands of the Spirit. He was filled with the Spirit and empty of selfishness and pride. That's when the power of God was poured out as thousands repented and were truly changed—to the glory of God—and the church exploded with passion and growth.

As pastors and leaders, we can insist on our agenda, or we can trust that God's agenda is best.

We all have a choice: to be like the Peter of the Gospels or like the Peter in Acts. The difference is a profound and life-changing encounter with Jesus. As pastors and leaders, we can insist on our agenda, or we can trust that God's agenda is best. If we believe His is the best, we need to listen, listen again, and then act on what He tells us.

A NEW COMMITMENT

Jesus said, "I do nothing on my own but speak just what the Father has taught me" (John 8:28). I made a vow to our church: "I will never again stand in this pulpit, or any other pulpit, and say anything that I haven't gotten from God."

Sometimes it has been very uncomfortable to wait for Him to speak to me and give me a message. (Remember, I'm a pretty organized guy.) But God has always come through to give me a message that's straight from Him.

I'm not saying that we shouldn't listen to other pastors and get ideas from them. That's part of the way the body of Christ operates. But when we listen to other pastors, we need to ask God what He wants us to teach and preach. If He says, "Yeah, tailor that talk for your church," then go for it. But if He says, "No, I have something else for you," listen and obey. Don't lean on other pastors; lean on God. Don't prepare your message and then ask God to bless it. Ask God for wisdom and direction for your message, then study and bathe your preparation in prayer.

Two weeks after God spoke to me about getting my messages from Him, I hosted a national conference of pastors of large churches. The entire purpose was for each of us to bring our three best sermon series outlines, videos, and graphics to share with each other. It was exactly what God had been telling me *not* to do, but the conference had been scheduled many months before. At the end of the event, I got up and told the group what the Lord had been saying to me about listening to Him first. Some were moved to tears, and a few got angry. That's okay. I had to be true to what God had said to me.

This is not an anti-intellectual approach. I'm not suggesting we throw out study and rely only on spontaneity. That's not it at all. I'm saying we should listen to the Lord, get direction from Him, and then study and pray like crazy to make the prophetic message as clear and powerful as possible. And we should listen to the best preachers in the land for inspiration, personal encouragement, and spiritual growth. In fact, we still have events for pastors to share their best messages with each other, but now we infuse our perspective, heart, and values into the event. We explain that the best way to be creative is to be vitally connected to the Creator. We begin by praying in the Spirit, and we tell people to only use the messages and concepts God puts on their hearts. Nothing else.

I'm saying we should listen to the Lord, get direction from Him, and then study and pray like crazy to make the prophetic message as clear and powerful as possible.

This approach pervades the leadership team at our church. I used to tell them every Tuesday about the topic I planned to preach and ask them for input. Now I ask them to pray and ask God what He wants to say to our church. The vast majority of the time, we come together after a week of prayer with the same topic on our hearts. The Lord may have given us different passages of Scripture, but this only makes worship richer and deeper. Often, Clayton comes in with a song he's written, and it fits perfectly with the message God has put on all our hearts. I tell you, it's a thrill to preach when you know God has spoken to and through your leadership team! It's no longer about our best ideas and our best plans. It's about God's heart, God's message, and God's desire to connect with every person who walks through our doors. This isn't us "doing church"; it's God-drenched, God-led, God-empowered, and God-ordained.

This approach has given me more confidence, more boldness, more humility, and more compassion than ever before. That's not a bad thing for a pastor—especially me!

Paul reminded the Corinthians where the marvel of truth comes from:

> No one's ever seen or heard anything like this,
> Never so much as imagined anything quite like it—
> What God has arranged for those who love him.
> But *you've* seen and heard it because God by his Spirit has brought it all out into the open before you.
> (1 Cor. 2:9, *The Message*)

Almost certainly, our preaching will change as God humbles us and restores us. This is a lesson I won't soon forget.

THINK ABOUT IT . . .

1. What are some signs that we are leading according to our agendas instead of God's?

2. What was the difference between the Peter of the Gospels and the Peter of Acts?

3. What is God saying to you about your submission, your pride and humility, and your preaching?

CHAPTER 8

BEHIND CLOSED DOORS

The new day wasn't just for our church. It was as much or more for me. One day I was praying, and I sensed the Lord tell me, "Be baptized in water." That was really strange because my father had baptized me in water when I was eight years old. I was confused. Why would God want me to do something that might cause people to question my salvation? It was weird. To make matters worse, my fourteen-year-old niece came up to me and asked, "Hey, Uncle Scott, how's your nervous breakdown going?"

I laughed and asked, "What in the world are you talking about, Kaylee?"

She smiled, "You know, the nervous breakdown you're having. You keep getting up and telling people how God is showing you all the stuff you've been doing wrong. Isn't that driving you crazy? I wondered how that's going for you."

She could tell I wasn't sure if she was serious, so she assured me, "I'm just joking with you, Uncle Scott. What you're doing is really powerful and honest."

Okay, my own niece thinks I'm nuts, and now God is telling me to get baptized. Everybody will be sure I've lost it! Then it hit me. Two weeks later, I was leading a trip to the Holy Land, and there's nothing strange about being baptized in the Jordan.

I had just completed the Freedom Quest weekend, and John had taken me through the twelve weeks of follow-up material to solidify my progress (more on that in Chapter 11). God was doing amazing things to set me free and give me a more passionate heart for Him. Being baptized, I realized, was a symbol that the old Scott had died and a new Scott had come alive. The old Scott who needed constant affirmation because he was insecure, the old Scott who trusted more in other pastors' insights than God's insights, the old Scott who had to control everything so he could look good needed to lie in a tomb. In his place, God was raising a new Scott to new life: one that was more secure, more free, more sensitive to the Spirit's voice, and more passionate about the right things than ever before. There was no going back. Baptism was the perfect symbol for the transformation God was doing in my life.

I called the team that was organizing the Holy Land tour to make sure we could arrange some time at the Jordan River for me to be baptized. A bunch of others on our trip wanted to be baptized there, too.

We flew all night to Tel Aviv. In the darkness of the plane, it looked like I was the only one awake. I sat there praying. I told the Lord, "I really believe You've spoken to me about getting baptized, but it would be really cool if You would confirm it." As a new spiritual discipline, I had been asking the Lord to put passages of Scripture in my mind. As soon as I asked God to confirm the impression, a biblical address popped into my head: Luke 12:50. I looked it up and read it. Jesus was telling His disciples, "But I have a baptism to undergo, and what constraint I am under until it is completed!" Jesus wasn't talking about water baptism. His baptism happened at the beginning of His ministry. He was talking about the baptism of His death to pay for sins—which was even more powerful to me, because I had already been baptized, and I was experiencing a kind of death to my own selfishness. In my solitude on the plane, I had an overwhelming sense of the presence of God. It was awesome!

Six days into the trip, we arrived at the place on the Jordan River where many people are baptized. But there was a problem. It was a holiday, and the place was closed. Our guide wasn't discouraged. He said, "I know a park that's always open. It's about a mile from the spot where Jesus was probably baptized." We were pumped!

A few minutes later, I was standing in the Jordan River with several board members and other close friends around me. I told them, "I don't want to be the old Scott I've been in the past. My immersion and coming up today symbolizes a new me, walking with the Spirit and empowered by the Spirit, totally devoted to the Father's will. I want to be like

Jesus, doing only what the Father tells me to do and saying only what the Father tells me to say." It was a glorious moment in my life.

But it wasn't the end of the transformation. If anything, it was only the beginning. As I've been more honest with God and open to Him, He has shown me far more refuse and twisted motives than I had ever seen before. In His strong and gentle hands, He has taken me through layer after layer, exposing sin and giving me more freedom, joy, and strength. It has been brutal and wonderful at the same time. Day after day, my pride has been crushed, but like grapes, the crushing has produced a delicious wine of gladness and intimacy with God.

Day after day, my pride has been crushed, but like grapes, the crushing has produced a delicious wine of gladness and intimacy with God.

A beautiful depiction of this kind of change is in C. S. Lewis's *Voyage of the Dawn Treader*. Eustace is a selfish boy who has found a fabulous treasure. He selfishly hoards what he has found, and goes to sleep with it. When he wakes up, he is no longer a boy; he's a dragon—an outward sign of his inner greed. He realizes he is cut off from his friends, and he weeps large dragon tears.

Aslan, the lion who is the symbol of Christ in these stories, shows up and leads Eustace to a garden on the top of a mountain. The boy-dragon is in pain from a gold bracelet he had put on when he was a boy but was now too tight on his big dragon arms. Eustace wants to get into a pool of water to soothe his pain, but Aslan tells him he has to get undressed first. With his claws, Eustace begins tearing his scaly skin. He peels off one layer only to discover another . . . and another. After three layers, he realizes his condition is hopeless. He can never get rid of his horrible skin by himself.

"You will have to let me undress you," said Aslan.

Eustace is afraid of Aslan, but he's also desperate. He lies down on his back. This is what he experienced:

> The very first tear he made was so deep that I thought it had gone right into my heart. And when he began pulling the skin off, it hurt worse than anything I've ever felt. The only thing that made me able to bear it was just the pleasure of feeling the stuff peel off. . . . Well, he peeled the beastly stuff right off—just as I thought I'd done it myself the other three times, only they hadn't hurt—and there it was lying on the grass: only ever so much thicker, and darker, and more knobbly-looking than the others had been. And there was I as smooth and soft as a peeled switch and smaller than I had been. Then he caught hold of me—I didn't like that much for I was very tender

> underneath now that I'd no skin on—and threw me into the water. It smarted like anything but only for a moment. After that it became perfectly delicious and as soon as I started swimming and splashing I found that all the pain had gone from my arm. And then I saw why. I'd turned into a boy again. . . . After a bit the lion took me out and dressed me . . . in new clothes.[7]

Eustace's experience perfectly describes the process God was taking me through. His scaly skin was a metaphor of my relationships with my family, my integrity, and my prayer life.

MY FAMILY

During this season of my life and ministry, John and I decided to take his son, Nehemiah, and my son, Dillon, to Haiti over spring break with one of our compassion ministries, Convoy of Hope. We went to several orphanages there. During the trip, Dillon and I experienced some tension. He was pushing back at me about all kinds of things, and I pushed back even harder. We acted more like competitive friends than a father and son. I hoped no one would notice, but I was sure John saw plenty!

When we got home, I took Jenni and the boys out to dinner. At the table that night, Dillon corrected me again about something so small neither of us can remember what it was. But it was one time too many. I barked, "Let me tell you something! You'd better shut your mouth. You'd better not correct me again, and you'd better show respect for me from this moment on. Do you understand me, son? I'm telling you, I'm done with it!"

Jenni's eyes were as big as saucers. You can imagine that dinner with the family that night wasn't the most pleasant experience of my life . . . or theirs. You could have cut the tension with a knife.

That night, Jenni and I talked until 2:00 in the morning. The pivotal moment occurred late in the conversation. I told her, "You see all that God is doing in me at church. It's incredible, but I'm not the man I need to be at home. I'm making a commitment to you tonight that *I will be* respected in our home."

Her voice got soft (which is a good indication that I need to listen), and she said, "Maybe you need to become a person worthy of our respect."

The next day I spoke with John about the scene at the restaurant and my talk with Jenni. He said, "Jenni's right. You know what the problem is, don't you?"

I must have looked confused because he didn't wait long for an answer. He continued, "Scott, your home is out of whack. You aren't the spiritual leader of your home."

"What do I do?" I asked.

"Go pray about it," he said. "The Lord will show you."

As I prayed, the Lord took me to the passage in Ephesians 5 about husbands and wives. It was crystal clear. It says,

> Husbands, love your wives, just as Christ loved the church and gave himself up for her to make her holy, cleansing her by the washing with water through the word, and to present her to himself as a radiant church, without stain or wrinkle or any other blemish, but holy and blameless. In this same way, husbands ought to love their wives as their own bodies. He who loves his wife loves himself. After all, no one ever hated their own body, but they feed and care for their body, just as Christ does the church. (Eph. 5:25–29)

The Lord asked me, "Are you praying for Jenni—like you mean it? Are you helping her with all the anxieties of being married to you and raising three sons? Are you nurturing her and nourishing her so that she is convinced that you delight in her? Are you speaking her love language? Are you cherishing her and protecting her so she feels completely safe and secure?"

Those questions weren't in a vacuum. The Lord reminded me of incidents (too many to count) when I hadn't been the husband I needed to be. A few weeks before these revelations, our phone rang in the middle of the night. I heard it, but I acted like I hadn't. Jenni answered it. It was my son, Hunter. He had gotten sick in his car, and he was asking for some help. The next morning, Jenni told me that she got up, dressed, and drove to meet Hunter in the middle of the night. She helped him clean up, and then she came back to the house.

When I told John about this (I hadn't confessed it to Jenni yet), he asked, "Why didn't you answer the phone and go help your son?"

I answered, "I was tired. I wanted to sleep."

Somehow, I sensed that my answer didn't have the ring of truth, love, and integrity! John looked at me for a couple of seconds and then said, "So, your need for rest was more important than Jenni's need for rest. Is that the way you see it?"

After dinner that evening, I asked my family to meet with me. I told them I hadn't been the servant leader of our home. I confessed that I hadn't loved them the way God wanted me to love them, that I'd had a double standard about what I watched on television and what I let others watch, and a number of my other failures as a husband and father. I took Jenni's advice. I asked them to forgive me, and I said, "I'm not going to demand that you respect me. I'm going to be the kind of husband and dad that is worthy of your respect. I'll earn it."

I began writing a devotional for them every day and sending it to them. Dakota is the only one of my boys who is young enough to still be at home. We found a couple of times every week to get together to talk about the devotional thoughts. I began praying not only *for* my wife and boys but also *with* them. When Dillon and Hunter are home, I gather them all so I can pray over them and ask God to bless and guide them.

Jenni has told people that the change in me has made all the difference in her world. For the first time she doesn't feel that she has four boys to take care of. Now she has a husband. I had been her "most compliant boy" because I did whatever she asked me to do, but I was still acting more like a boy—a spoiled boy at that—than the strong and loving husband I needed to be. That was changing. People who attended The Oaks on Sunday morning had seen a big change in my leadership, but now Jenni and the boys were seeing real change behind closed doors.

People who attended The Oaks on Sunday morning had seen a big change in my leadership, but now Jenni and the boys were seeing real change behind closed doors.

INTEGRITY

Some people lie because they're afraid of losing the approval of others, and other people lie because the truth is inconvenient. I've lied for both reasons. Of course, I didn't call them lies. They were exaggerations, hyperbole, or selective truth. If something was pretty good, I often embellished the story to make it a little better. If it was bad, I either made the story a little worse to gain sympathy, or I minimized the problem so I wouldn't appear so much at fault. Why did I do those things? To impress people with the good and to get out of trouble when I looked bad. I shaded the truth for such a long time that it became second nature . . . until my good friend John and the Holy Spirit ganged up on me in love.

About a year ago, I was invited to attend a leadership conference and speak about what God was doing at The Oaks. One morning when I was meeting with John, I said, "Wouldn't it be cool for you to go with me?"

He smiled and nodded, "Yeah, I guess so."

I told him, "I'll call the event director and work it out. It'll be great!"

An hour or two later, I called the gentleman and said, "My friend John Bates would love to come to the conference. Would that be okay?" Instantly, I realized I made it sound like John had requested an invitation. I wanted to clarify my comment, but the words of retraction wouldn't come.

The next day I told John about my talk with the director. I tried to rush through it so he didn't notice anything, but he stopped me. He said, "Whoa. Wait, Scott. That's not the way it happened. You invited me. I didn't invite myself. You've put me in an awkward position." He paused for a second and then said, "You know you're going to have to make that right, don't you?"

I wanted to vanish from the room, but I was still sitting there. I knew I had to call the director. I told him, "I misrepresented my conversation with John. He didn't ask to come. I suggested it, and then I told you in a way that wasn't completely accurate. It's not his idea to go. It was entirely mine. Please forgive me."

John wanted to be sure the director got the message, so he also called and the director said, "Scott called me today to be sure I knew the truth about the trip. We're all clear. No problem."

I wish this was the only example of my need to repent of shading the truth for my benefit, but it's not. Gradually, I've become more sensitive to my tendency to exaggerate or misrepresent situations, so now I'm better able to limit myself to the complete truth before I've sinned. That's real progress! I have years of habits to overcome, but the Spirit and John are gang tackling me. Change is happening.

MY PRAYER LIFE

One day I talked to John about my sons. I told him I was wrestling with some fears about their future. They weren't dealing drugs or anything like that, but I knew the temptations every young man faces—and it concerned me.

John asked, "What does the Word of God say about those fears?"

I shrugged, "I'm not sure."

He explained, "We have spiritual weapons of prayer, but too often, they are like pistols without bullets. We need the ammunition of a prophetic word—the power to demolish strongholds. You need a prophetic word for each of your sons."

That sounded good, but I wasn't sure what to do next. I asked, "Okay, I'm in, but what do I do?"

He looked at me like Jesus must have looked at Philip when he asked Him to show them the Father. John kind of shook his head and said, "What do you think? Pray about it."

I asked God to give me a word for Dillon, Hunter, and Dakota, and He did. It was wonderful. My prayers became clear, directed, powerful, and confident. I stopped badgering them about changes I wanted to see in their lives, and I began trusting that God would fulfill the word He had given me in His way and in His time. I prayed those prophetic words for them for about four months before I told them what God had given me for them.

The principle applies to every area of life:

- Identify the area of anxiety, worry, or concern. Don't minimize it or deny it.
- Ask God for a prophetic word as ammo for your prayers.
- Pray the prophetic word—and the Word of God—in faith, believing that God will accomplish all He has promised to do.

- Watch for signs that the Lord is at work. Certainly, we can see only a billionth of what God is up to, but even a glimpse is enough to encourage us. If we'll look with an expectant heart, we will often see His hand at work, and our hearts will be flooded with gratitude.

We can see only a billionth of what God is up to, but even a glimpse is enough to encourage us.

All the messages to the seven churches in the opening chapters of Revelation are first to the "angel," which refers to the messenger, the leader, the pastor. He or she has to be transformed first, and then the pastor's family, church, and community will have someone worth following.

If you want a new day at your church, if you want to clear the stage for the Spirit of God to do what only He can do, then be ready for a personal baptism of death and resurrection. The things that need to perish may die painful and bloody deaths, yet the process is necessary. But there's always hope in a glorious resurrection of a new person with more intimacy with God, more humility and spiritual power, and more love for everyone.

Make no mistake: it's uncomfortable to "die daily." It's a lot easier to hide behind self-protection, continue playing games with the truth to impress people or avoid criticism, and maintain the status quo. But if you play it safe, you'll miss out on the adventure of seeing God enter your life and your ministry in a way you've never experienced before.

As God has been working in me, people have noticed. Jenni, my sons, our team, our friends, our elders, and every person who knows me well have said they see more joy, peace, and confidence in me than they've ever seen before. When I'm in the center of God's plan and purposes instead of insisting on my ways and my control, I can relax. I don't have to prove anything, and I don't feel compelled to promote myself. I can relax, and I can pour myself into others without always thinking about what I'll gain by helping them. I can walk in confidence, which gives me a beautiful combination of excitement and rest. I'm very much still a work in progress, but I keep trying to move forward.

The new day doesn't just happen in the pastor's public world; it happens—maybe even more profoundly—behind closed doors.

THINK ABOUT IT . . .

1. What would a new day look like for you and your relationships in your family? Your small group? Your ministry team?

2. What would it look like in regard to your sense of integrity (honesty and consistency)?

3. What would it look like in your prayer life to have the ammo of the prophetic word?

CHAPTER 9

THE LEAD FOLLOWER

For years, I had an agenda—for my leaders, for my staff, for my church, and for my career. I was sure my agenda was in the ballpark of God's will. I was talking about Jesus, leading people to faith in Him, and building a great ministry. We had programs of all colors and stripes that were creative and effective. We built buildings, sent out missionaries, cared for the poor, equipped young ministers, and all the rest. At every point and in every moment, the measuring stick was growth—especially compared to other churches. We were, I thought, doing pretty well. What more could anyone do for God?

I struggled with the conflict between being the boss of the church and my goal to help God build His kingdom. I saw my role as making things happen for God. Where did my responsibility start and stop? What was God's job, after all? All of this was very confusing, but I tried to avoid thinking about it too much.

I don't think I'm the only one. As I've talked with pastors, it seems that we're the most insecure people on earth!

We constantly are faced with the fact (or the fear) that we lack education, talent, time, money, people, and other resources to get the job done. We're sure we'll take the hit when anything goes wrong—which is a certainty sooner or later. We put on a happy face, but under the mask we're often consumed with doubt and fear.

SINK YOURSELF INTO THAT

In Paul's letter to the Galatians, he addressed their theology, their racial prejudice, and their bickering with each other. (It seems things in their church were similar to many of our churches today!) Envy and comparison were destroying relationships. Near the end of the letter, he told them to resolve conflict through forgiveness and to care for one another. He knew they would never find peace and power if they kept checking out where they were on the pecking order. He wrote,

> Make a careful exploration of who you are and the work you have been given, and then sink yourself into that. Don't be impressed with yourself. Don't compare yourself with others. Each of you must take responsibility for doing the creative best you can with your own life. (Gal. 6:4–5, *The Message*)

Essentially, every message in the world—on billboards, on popular radio stations, in magazines, in shop windows, and in everyday conversations—tells us that true fulfillment comes through success, pleasure, and approval. It's a lie. No amount of money, fame, applause, comfort, or power can fill the God-shaped hole in our hearts. Only God can fill it. It's no different for pastors, except that we often preach the truth about our only hope while we continue to pursue success, pleasure, and approval to meet our deepest needs.

Paul encouraged the Galatians, and us, to make a careful analysis of what makes us tick. What do we daydream about? What thrills us? What ruins our day? When we find the deep, deep love of God and His calling in our lives, we need to sink ourselves into that. Then we won't be too impressed with ourselves, we won't let comparison make us feel inferior or superior, and we'll have a new way of thinking about our God-given calling.

When we find the deep, deep love of God and His calling in our lives, we need to sink ourselves into that.

Earlier in Paul's letter, he explained that the foundation of our identity isn't in our performance, but in our adoption into God's family. Many of us live on a rollercoaster of emotions: we feel euphoric when we're succeeding, and we're depressed when things aren't going well. There's another way. We can be thrilled all the time that we belong to God. Paul wrote that the gospel of Christ has set us free from slavery to sin:

> We have been set free to experience our rightful heritage. You can tell for sure that you are now fully adopted as his own children because God sent the Spirit of his Son into our lives crying out, "Papa! Father!" Doesn't that privilege of intimate conversation with God make it plain that you are not a slave, but a child? And if you are a child, you're also an heir, with complete access to the inheritance. (Gal. 4:3–7, *The Message*)

Our performance may be wonderful or terrible, but our adoption is still secure. People's responses may be wonderful or terrible, but God's love for us never wavers an inch. No matter what, we belong to our Father.

One major component of identity is a person's name. Names don't mean as much today as they did many years ago, but if we dig, we might find something meaningful. One day John and I met, and he asked me what my middle name is. I told him it's Scott. He said, "No, your middle name."

"That *is* my middle name," I assured him.

"Then what's your first name?"

"Do I have to tell you?" I asked.

"It can't be that bad!"

"Okay," I almost whispered. "It's Wyndell."

He almost shouted, "Wyndell?"

"See, I told you. My grandfather's name was Wyndell Claudell. That's why he told everybody to call him W. C."

John checked a website he had on his laptop. He said, "I'm going to see what your name means." After a few seconds, he reported, "'Wyndell' means 'messenger of truth.' 'Scott' means 'temple of God.' And 'Wilson' means 'noble spirit.'"

John paused for a second, and then he told me, "Scott, it wasn't simply your parents giving you these names. They are prophetic words from God about your identity and your role in the kingdom. When people speak your name, they're reaffirming the word God has given concerning you. You are a messenger of truth, you are the temple of God, and you have a noble spirit."

I thought that was really cool, but John seldom leaves things one-dimensional. After a few seconds, he said, "What's the opposite of those traits?"

We explored the idea for a while, and we realized the Enemy's biggest attacks in my life are to counteract my identity. I struggle with truth, defiling the temple of God with unclean thoughts, and having a peasant mentality of inferiority. Suddenly, a lot of things became clear!

In our new identity as God's children, we're called to participate in the family business. What is God's business? To seek and save the lost, redeem a broken world, and restore families, friends, and nations. We don't have to wonder what our roles are. We have the Great Commandment to love God with all our hearts and our neighbors as ourselves. We also have the Great Commission to live in the authority of the risen Christ and go to the ends of the earth to make disciples who love Him. What an incredible honor to be a son or daughter working alongside our Father and Jesus our brother in the power of the Spirit!

What an incredible honor to be a son or daughter working alongside our Father and Jesus our brother in the power of the Spirit!

What's the business plan? Again, it's not hard to uncover.

Watch what the Father is doing and copy Him.

Jesus told His disciples, "I'm telling you this straight. The Son can't independently do a thing, only what he sees the Father doing. What the Father does, the Son does. The Father loves the Son and includes him in everything he is doing" (John 5:19–20, *The Message*).

Listen, and say what the Father is saying.

Jesus explained, "Don't you believe that I am in the Father, and that the Father is in me? The words I say to you I do not speak on my own authority. Rather, it is the Father, living in me, who is doing his work" (John 14:10).

Believe the Father loves you as much as He loves Jesus.

Jesus prayed for His disciples and for all the believers who would respond to their message: "You sent me and have loved them even as you have loved me" (John 17:23).

DON'T BE IMPRESSED WITH YOURSELF

We have a new identity as children of God, but this understanding makes us more dependent, not less. Our fallen human natures have been crucified, but they take time to die. Our task is to continue to crucify our sinful passions every time they arise—which is pretty often! We can't manufacture true spiritual fruit. The production of this fruit is a process that requires continual connection with the source of nourishment, the Holy Spirit and the holy Word of God.

DON'T COMPARE YOURSELF WITH OTHERS

When we read the accounts of Jesus' life, we realize He was a lightning rod. People either loved Him or hated Him; no one thought He was "just okay." It's easy to become consumed and distracted by criticism or praise. They can make us take our eyes off the Lord and put them on the people who oppose us, or on our accomplishments. We need to receive both through the grid of grace, accepting criticism as possibly a word from the Lord for our correction (even if it comes from an angry person), accepting praise as a gift from the Lord, and then giving it all to Him.

Criticism or adulation never distracted Jesus. Sometimes people were so impressed that they wanted to crown Him king. At other times, they wanted to kill Him. In a remarkable scene in Matthew's Gospel, the writer tells us,

> Jesus, knowing they were out to get him, moved on. A lot of people followed him, and he healed them all.

He also cautioned them to keep it quiet, following guidelines set down by Isaiah:

"Look well at my handpicked servant;
  I love him so much, take such delight in him.
I've placed my Spirit on him;
  he'll decree justice to the nations.
But he won't yell, won't raise his voice;
  there'll be no commotion in the streets.
He won't walk over anyone's feelings,
  won't push you into a corner.
Before you know it, his justice will triumph;
  the mere sound of his name will signal hope, even
  among far-off unbelievers." (Matt. 12:15–21,
  The Message)

As we follow Christ, we can follow His example in handling criticism and praise. Here are some benchmarks that parallel what Matthew is reminding us:

Are you confident that . . .

- the Father has handpicked you?
- the Father loves you perfectly?
- the Father takes delight in you apart from your performance?
- the Father has placed His Spirit in you?
- the Father's message is truth?

If you believe this, then you don't have to . . .

- yell or raise your voice.
- worry about getting everything right.
- worry about people finding out you're not perfect.
- start a commotion to get attention or control people.
- step on anyone's feelings.
- push people around.

A NEW ROLE, A NEW TITLE

As I've experienced the new day in my life and our church, I've seen my role from an entirely different perspective. I already alluded to it earlier in the book. For a long time, I saw myself as indispensable to the life of our church. I worked hard, and I hoped everyone noticed. When we grew, I made sure people noticed! When we suffered setbacks, I always had a ready excuse. But now, I realize I'm not really the leader of our church; God is. He's in charge. It's His message, His people, His cause, and His process. I'm just a follower. My role as pastor makes me the "Lead Follower," but I'm still simply a follower. My main job is to get my directions from the top, and trust Him to work in and through me. That's enough, and that's just right.

THINK ABOUT IT . . .

1. What does it mean to "sink yourself into" your identity as God's beloved child? What difference would it make? How would it help you get off the emotional rollercoaster?

2. How does it transform your life and leadership to see yourself as a junior partner in God's family business?

3. How do criticism and adulation distract us? How can the principles in Matthew 12:15–21 be the antidote?

SECTION 4

THE ROLLOUT

(JOHN'S VOICE)

CHAPTER 10
THE CORE

When we, as pastors and church leaders, clear the stage for the Holy Spirit to work powerfully in our services, we open doors to both privilege and responsibility. We have the great privilege of watching God do amazing things in the lives of people. As the gifts are expressed, people experience the presence and love of God, they sense His forgiveness and cleansing, they find new direction in hard times, broken relationships are mended, confused people find truth, and discouraged people experience new hope. It's glorious!

Leadership, though, requires us to teach, train, and shepherd people so our churches don't become either complacent or chaotic. We are responsible to impart sound teaching, equip mentors, and provide environments where people can grow in the knowledge of God and can practice the gifts. We aren't offering a particular prescription of how churches need to create this kind of environment. However, our experience has been instructive.

Clearing the stage is an absolutely crucial first step, but only the first one of many. Environments of committed and passionate prayer, spiritual breakthroughs, sound teaching, and mentoring relationships can take many forms. I want to describe the environments God has led us to create at Freedom Fellowship International. I'll begin with the most important one: building a team of people who pray passionately.

At our church, the Core is a group of people radically committed to pray that the Spirit of God would do His mighty work in and through the people of Freedom Fellowship International and beyond. These people are thoroughly convinced that only God can change lives, and they persistently beat on the gates of heaven to ask God to do the impossible. They are part of a comprehensive strategy God has given us:

- A select group of men and women committed to radical prayer: the Core
- An event designed to help people break through the strongholds of sin, fear, and doubt in their lives: Freedom Quest
- A follow-up series for mentors to impart spiritual principles and practices to the people who attended the event
- A School of Supernatural Ministry, designed to equip people to flow in the gifts of the Spirit

The centerpiece of this strategy—the part that undergirds and holds it all together—is concerted, passionate, directed, Spirit-filled prayer. This commitment to prayer, though, has to begin with the pastor. At our church, it begins with me.

As I look back over my life, the most important lessons I've learned are about hearing, knowing, and obeying the voice of God. My wife, Shelli, and I both come from a family lineage of ministry. I grew up in a pastor's home, and my grandfather was a pastor. Shelli's background is virtually the same. We were, as the saying goes, "brought up in the church." Unfortunately, we were so familiar with "how to do ministry" that we didn't need God to make it happen. We knew how to put a service together and which programs would work. We had a sixth sense about what would upset particular people and what would bring visitors back the next week. We became experts in spiritual anthropology: we knew how people would react to every situation. With these insights, every aspect of our ministry was carefully planned and orchestrated—and it seemed to work.

In my early years of ministry, I had the opportunity to serve in some large churches. I assumed I was destined to be the pastor of a megachurch, but it didn't work out the way I planned. When a church near Dallas invited me to be their pastor, there were forty-four people attending. Shelli and I were the two youngest people among the members.

The large churches where I'd served were creative and innovative. I assumed I would go to a church where I could try some new things, but my new church was traditional . . . *very* traditional. Almost anything creative made them feel uncomfortable, which made me feel uncomfortable. However, discomfort shouldn't rule over practice. In *Worship His Majesty,* Jack Hayford writes, "Tradition must be confronted and questioned and adjustments made if God's maximum benefits are to be realized during worship."[8]

God has a way of getting our attention. A little more than two years into my time at the church, we experienced severe leadership conflict. Our church had grown to more than 200, but some of the board members were upset with my leadership. They told me it was time for me to go. I was devastated. I believed this was the end of my time at the church, but even more, for me as a pastor.

One day as I sat praying in the church, I imagined what it must have been like for David as he ran from the army of King Saul. I felt attacked, misunderstood, and pursued by people who would have loved to see my head on a stick! I could feel my heart skipping beats. I actually wondered if I would survive this calamity in our church's life . . . in *my* life.

In desperation, I went to a small revival service to see if God might speak to me and give me some direction. During the service, a man gave me a prophetic word: "God says your situation at the church will be healed by the end of the year. He will give you a new hunger for Him, and He will use you in a way that's broader than just your local church."

I really didn't believe him, but I tried to accept it as a word from God. Within minutes, the Lord's encouragement penetrated the hard shell I had built around my heart. I cried a lot throughout the rest of the night.

In the next few days, I realized my heart had drifted far from God. Before the conflict with our leaders, I had depended on my experience more than the Spirit to make the church run. During the tense time with our board, I tried to protect my heart by drawing away from any vulnerability, with people and with God. I realized it was time to draw near to God, to learn to listen to His voice.

I realized it was time to draw near to God, to learn to listen to His voice.

LEARNING TO LISTEN

Let's take a step back to look at how God communicates with His people. From the cradle to the grave, our public preaching and private teaching reinforce the truth that God offers us a relationship with Him based on grace. A relationship always implies communication. Without the give and take of communication, it's difficult to imagine a meaningful relationship. In our relationship with God, we might identify three overlapping ways He communicates with us.

First, God has given us His Word. All Scripture, Paul tells us, is "God-breathed" (2 Tim. 3:16). And Peter reminds us that every word from God is prophetic: "Above all, you must understand that no prophecy of Scripture came about by the prophet's own interpretation of things. For prophecy never had its origin in the human will, but prophets, though human, spoke from God as they were carried along by the Holy Spirit" (2 Peter 1:20–21). In his work, *Knowing the Holy Spirit Through the Old Testament,* Christopher Wright refers to this passage and observes, "Peter tells us here that the prophets of the Old Testament did not make up their own messages out of their heads or imaginations. Rather, he affirms the double authorship of the Scriptures: 'Men spoke from God.' It was human beings who did the speaking, but it was God who provided the message."[9]

But the Word of God isn't just marks on paper. In one of the most magnificent pieces of literature ever penned, John tells us, "In the beginning was the Word, and the Word was with God, and the Word was God," and, "The Word became flesh and made his dwelling among us. We have seen his glory, the glory of the one and only Son, who came from the Father, full of grace and truth" (John 1:1, 14). Jesus told His companions on the road to Emmaus that all of the Old Testament points to Him. The writer to the Hebrews takes up this concept: "In the past God spoke to our ancestors through the prophets at many times and in various ways, but in these last days he has spoken to us by his Son, whom he appointed heir of all things, and through whom also he made the universe" (Heb. 1:1–2). The primary, clearest, and most powerful way God has spoken to us is through the written and incarnate Word.

The primary, clearest, and most powerful way God has spoken to us is through the written and incarnate Word.

Second, God speaks to us by reminding us what the Scriptures say. Over and over again in the Bible, the Lord reminds us to remember. The Spirit brings passages to mind as we ask Him to remind us and as we need them. Jesus lived a Scripture-drenched life. Again and again, He quoted Scripture. At the outset of His ministry, He quoted Isaiah's prediction of the role of the Messiah. During His ministry, He often used themes familiar to His listeners. When He talked about being a "good shepherd" in John 10, every person hearing Him would instantly think of "the LORD is my shepherd" in Psalm 23. After He told the woman at the well that He could give her "living water," the people she told would immediately recognize His reference to Jeremiah's warning:

> "My people have committed two sins:
> They have forsaken me,
> the spring of living water,

and have dug their own cisterns,
broken cisterns that cannot hold water." (Jer. 2:13)

And at the end as He hung on the cross, Jesus cried out the words of David from Psalm 22: "My God, my God, why have you forsaken me?"

The Lord wants to bring the Scriptures to mind for us, too, to assure us of His affection, to guide us when we're confused, and to strengthen us when we're weak. But passages of Scripture don't come to mind if they aren't first deposited there. We have to get the first things first—to know the Word so the Spirit can remind us of the Word when we're in need.

Third, God wants to speak to us as a loving parent talks to a child, or a friend to a friend, with words spoken to our hearts. We may want this to be the dominant way God speaks to us, but we will seldom hear these intimate and special words if we haven't become familiar with the truth of Scripture and experiences of the Spirit reminding us of particular passages when we need them.

When I was at that pivotal point in my spiritual life, I knew a lot of Scripture. I'd studied and memorized many passages for preaching and teaching, and God had used many of those to remind me of His love and purpose. Now it was time to learn the third way of listening and obeying. For about two months, I walked around outside our neighborhood after dinner and listened for the voice of God. I needed to distinguish His voice from the voice of the Enemy and my own voice. It wasn't easy. I wasn't accustomed to this level of discernment. Almost every night during those months, I listened for God to whisper directions to me. They were often very simple: turn this way, go here, or say that. I analyzed each of them, and gradually, His voice became clearer. It was similar to dog obedience school: repetition, repetition, repetition. Each time I obeyed, I felt a sense of God's presence and peace. When I resisted or attempted to explain it away, I had a feeling that something was missing, so I returned and did what I sensed God was telling me to do. Then I felt His presence and peace.

Submission and obedience aren't disconnected concepts. There is no true obedience without a submissive heart. Our human nature resists submission. We want to be in control of our own lives, and we trust our wisdom more than God's. It's a fool's game. We may smile and play the game at church so people think we're devoted Christians, but a selfish, unbelieving heart has a way of raising its ugly head. The solution? A genuine, soul-wrenching, heartwarming encounter with the living God.

There is no true obedience without a submissive heart.

In *Spiritual Authority*, Watchman Nee commented, "A man who is rebellious in his heart will soon utter rebellious words, for out of the abundance of the heart the mouth speaks. To know authority, one must first meet authority; otherwise he will never obey. The mere hearing of the message of obedience is totally ineffective. He must have an encounter with God; then the foundation of God's authority will be laid in his life."[10]

Jesus explained that sheep hear and understand their shepherd's voice (John 10:4). I've been in the Middle East, and I've seen a particular group of sheep in a seemingly hopelessly mixed flock respond to a man's voice to follow him. I was learning to hear and understand my Shepherd's voice, too. I don't have a perfect record. Far from it. Sometimes I'm too busy to listen, sometimes I'm confused by what I hear, and sometimes I just don't want to do what I sense God is leading me to do. When I refuse to obey God's voice, I'm miserable, and my people miss out on the flow of the Spirit's blessing. My defiance is saying, "I know better than You do, God, how my life should work." That's arrogance; that's idolatry, putting myself in the place of God.

Over the years, there have been many occasions when the Lord told me to do something specific, usually something very simple like taking off my tie during a service. Each time, God used it in the lives of people in our church to confirm something He was saying to them.

On a few occasions, I've really blown it. A few years after I began learning to listen and obey, our church suffered severe financial problems. As I prayed, the Lord told me to inform our board that I wasn't going to receive a salary for a year. Shelli was pregnant with our second child, and we were barely making ends meet. It seemed totally unreasonable—and irresponsible—to forego a paycheck. But the Lord assured me that if I would obey Him, He would take care of us.

I went home after work to talk to Shelli. When I arrived, she told me she needed to go to the store to buy some last minute things for the baby's room. We were having a daughter this time, and Shelli was excited about having a baby girl in the house. Before I could say anything to her, our youth pastor drove up and parked behind Shelli's car.

I walked Shelli out to the car. Before she closed the door, I said, "I need to talk to you about something."

She said, "It needs to be quick. I have to run to the store and be right back."

I took a deep breath. "You know, our church is having financial problems." She looked at me like I was as dense as a board. Of course she knew. I continued, "The Lord spoke to me and told me not to take a salary for a year."

Her expression changed. She shook her head and said, "That's crazy. The Lord wouldn't tell you something like that—not at this point in our lives!"

I nodded, but she shot back. "It can't be. It makes no sense!" She put the car in reverse and backed into the youth pastor's car. *Boom*!

It was the straw that broke the camel's back. I hadn't picked the best time to drop a bomb on my wife. The whole thing had blown up in an instant. She thought I was nuts, and I had caused her to get so upset she had a wreck . . . in our driveway.

I told God, "I'm sorry. I can't do this." The next year or so were grueling at our church. The financial strains were extremely painful, and worse, I lived with the nagging knowledge that I hadn't obeyed God.

About three years later I went to a pastors' conference in Arkansas. There, I heard a young pastor named Bryan Jarrett, who told a story of faith. His church was having financial difficulties, his wife was pregnant, and the Lord told him, "If you'll do without a salary for a year, I'll pay off your church's debt and take care of you and your family."

When Bryan told his wife, Haley, what God said to him, she replied, "I trust you. We'll do what God told you to do." And God did exactly what He promised to do. Seemingly out of nowhere, trucks showed up at his house with a freezer, a load of frozen food, a baby bed, and all kinds of other things. During the entire year, God miraculously provided for Bryan and his family. And just as miraculously, the church's debt was paid off.

As I sat listening to Bryan, the Lord said to me, "That's what I had planned for you three years ago." I wept. I had missed God's blessing for me, for my family, and for our church. And I was angry—not at Shelli for questioning and resisting, but at myself for not being the kind of husband whose wife would trust him implicitly. It was my fault, not hers. I prayed, "Lord, please give me another chance. If You ask me to do something else crazy again, I'll do it."

I didn't hear any strange directions from God for about eight years. Then, in 2011, our church was involved in raising funds for a ministry to help the poor. As I talked to our people about their sacrifice to meet this need, I told them to pray and ask God what He would have them do.

Shelli and I had already decided what we were going to give, but I asked God again for directions. This time, He said, "Give away every shirt, jacket, pair of pants, and pair of shoes you own—except one shirt, one pair of pants, one belt, one pair of socks, one set of underwear, and shoes. Everything. And don't buy anything for a year."

I had a lot of clothes, so this seemed harder than not taking a salary for a year! After running the plan by my mentor Doc Lee, I told Shelli, and she thought it was a great direction from God. I had earned more of her trust during the previous decade. We didn't tell anyone else, but they would find out soon enough when my wardrobe selections looked like *Groundhog Day*!

Before I told anyone besides Shelli, a lady in our church came up to me and said the Lord told her I was going to have a new wardrobe of the finest clothes, even designer clothes. I smiled and nodded, but I was sure she was completely wrong.

A few days later at a banquet, I told my story and put all my clothes on racks and in boxes. From that moment on, they were no longer mine. The next day, a Saturday, a friend came over to help me load a truck with all my clothes. I was left with only the outfit I expected to be wearing for the next fifty-two weeks. After we finished, he said, "I wonder if you'd go somewhere with me."

I didn't have anything else to do. I asked, "Where do you want to go?"

"Shopping. Shopping for clothes," he announced.

That was the last thing I wanted to do! I winced and tried to find words to get out of going. He then explained, "I'm going to buy you some clothes."

"No," I corrected him. I guess he hadn't been listening to my story the night before. "These are the clothes I'm going to wear for a year."

He smiled, "Didn't you say the Lord told you that *you* couldn't buy any clothes?"

I was wary, but I nodded.

"But He didn't say *I* can't buy you any clothes, did He?"

We went to the store where he bought me a new wardrobe: socks, belts, shirts, pants, shoes, two jackets, underwear, workout gear . . . the works. But that wasn't the end of it. Other people bought me the finest clothes, ones I would never have bought for myself . . . the kind the lady in our church said the Lord had promised to provide. I guess she wasn't so wrong after all.

During that season, the Lord touched people's hearts to give generously, and the idea spread throughout the community. Cash and clothes for the poor came from everywhere. We couldn't give them away fast enough to keep up with all that was being donated.

In a month, the Lord provided a wealth of clothes for poor people. And for a (finally) obedient pastor, He gave twenty-two pairs of pants, twenty-seven shirts, four sweaters, three suits and ties, eight belts, sixteen pairs of shoes, three coats, and all kinds of other things—articles of clothing I'll never again take for granted because it was abundantly obvious that God had provided them. It was such an adventure, such a thrill!

Obedience opens the doors to God's blessings. I can't wait to hear from God again when He leads me to do something crazy. Radical expectancy has become the theme of my life. The delight of my life is to know, hear, and obey God.

Radical expectancy has become the theme of my life. The delight of my life is to know, hear, and obey God.

PEOPLE WHO PRAY

When I arrived at the church where I'm a pastor today, they had a regular prayer meeting every Saturday night from 6:00 to 7:00. It was traditional . . . and very dry. Every week, a faithful few came in and found their regular places. They were faithful people, but not passionate people—because no one had lit a fire in them. We played some soft organ music, and in an hour we were done. There was no interaction and no displays of spiritual presence or power.

After Dr. Wayne Lee came as a consultant to help our church develop a ministry of powerful and passionate prayer, I learned some important lessons about building a fireplace and inviting the Spirit to send His fire. It's all about prayer. Gradually we developed a gathering of radically committed men and women who understand what it means to pray "in the Spirit."

Let me outline the principles and practices of our Core. We still have a one-hour prayer meeting on Saturday nights from 6:00 to 7:00 because we respect people's time. But we also respect the work of the Spirit, so our goal and activities are Spirit-filled, Spirit-led, and Spirit-empowered.

We follow a model we call GROW Prayer, with the acrostic standing for:

Gathering

We begin by praying in the Spirit, all of us, loudly, demonstratively, and passionately, holding nothing back. People share words of wisdom and prophetic words from the Lord. Their gifts are on high alert, and they get to use them for the sake of others. It's a soul-satisfying time.

Redemption

This segment focuses on specific needs in our church, our network of churches, and around the world. It isn't a time for people to ask others to pray for personal needs. We're there to represent the needs of others, not ourselves. There are plenty of opportunities for us to share our needs in other venues.

Omnipotence

We spend time praying about seemingly impossible situations, where answers can only come about through the intervention of a mighty God. We aren't shy about asking God to work in miraculous ways.

Worship

We end with a strategic time of asking God to align our hearts with His. We focus on His attributes: His majesty, His kindness and acceptance, the work of the cross, His power, and His wisdom. We long for God's will and His ways above all else—or at least, we long to long for Him above all else. Drawing close to God often reveals areas where His Spirit needs to work in us. We leave with a powerful sense of God's love and power, and we expect Him to answer the prayers we've brought to Him.

Each of these segments lasts approximately fifteen minutes. If you try something similar in your own church, it's important to keep things moving. When people become bored or lost in thought, they become disengaged. In praise and petitions, every part of us needs to be actively engaged. In every endeavor, engaged people are enthusiastic people. The last thing our people need is one more boring, ineffective prayer meeting.

The people attending already have a heart for prayer, so don't be afraid to challenge them to pray out loud and even walk around as they pray. Some of the most demonstrative prayers happen at Jerusalem's Wailing Wall. Don't allow your prayer partners to disconnect their minds, souls (emotions), spirits, and bodies. We worship God "in spirit and in truth." In worship I often find myself silent and still in His presence. My spirit is connecting with God's Spirit. I learned a few important lessons:

- Don't underestimate the power of music to accompany prayer, especially during the segments of Gathering (upbeat) and Worship (reflective).
- As leaders arise, let them assist in leading different parts of the prayer hour. Letting them lead inspires their ownership.
- At the end of the hour, I always pray a prayer of blessing over the participants and thank them for being a part of our prayer team.

- Of course, we have an agreement that everything said in the room is strictly confidential. Our trust in one another, and the church's trust in each of us, is based on our commitment to confidentiality.
- We also have formed smaller teams out of our larger group of people who are committed to pray for specific concerns during the week. Some focus on new church plants. For instance, they might pray for a new church in Kentucky. The Lord gives them prophetic words for the pastor and the people at the church, and one of our people sends those words to encourage and guide them. Another group prays prophetically for Scott and The Oaks. We actually made this commitment before Scott and I began meeting together regularly. One group serves as the prayer covering for the staff at the national office of our denominational fellowship. Another prays for the "top five" needs of our church—whatever is on our hearts that week. And finally, a group of people prays around the clock for my family and me, and I didn't even need to ask. A lady in our church had a vision and a burden to provide this support for us. God bless her.

When we began this ministry of prayer years ago, about forty people joined us. We now have one hundred, and it's still growing.

HONESTY AND FREEDOM

The level of our honesty—first the pastor's, and then the others'—determines the level of freedom, joy, and power for our church. I'm committed to being completely, absolutely honest with God about my deepest hopes, fears, sins, and desires. I'm also committed to being honest with my mentor. If I don't tell him what's really going on in my heart, he can't speak truth into it. Other than my mentor and Shelli, I try to be careful about sharing the junk in my life with others. I need to ask God if, when, and how He wants me to share with our prayer team and/or our congregation. It doesn't help them, and it doesn't honor them, for me to air my dirty laundry without any spiritual filters. (Generally, the questions about disclosure are: Does it implicate anyone else? Does it shame anyone else? Has God worked sufficiently in me so that I've seen genuine progress in this issue? Am I using it for shock value, personal therapy, or to help others walk with God? Is this the right time? Have I gotten good advice from wise mentors and trusted friends?)

We eagerly desire for everyone to engage in the gifts of the Spirit in all of our prayer meetings. We pray loudly, and we pray in tongues. There are no strangers among us who might be confused, so we encourage each person to let the Spirit flow.

This group of praying people has raised the level of every element of the church. Before we do anything, we pray about it—and I mean *pray* about it. Half-hearted people need not apply. These folks are serious . . . and joyful. We ask God for wisdom, and we trust Him for favor.

Asking God for favor isn't just magical thinking. It's not getting a parking spot in the front row of the grocery store. God may not have opened that parking spot for me at all. Maybe, just maybe, He wanted me to pass it by so an elderly person could park there, and maybe, just maybe, He wanted me to park in the back so I could get a little exercise. No, the favor of God isn't in getting the trivial things we want.

The favor of God is the revelation of two things: the will of God and the plan of the Enemy. When we grasp truth from His Word or get a word of knowledge, wisdom, or prophecy, we can then make wise, Spirit-led decisions and please the One who bought us. That's the favor of the Lord, and that's what we expect to receive during our times of prayer.

The favor of God is the revelation of two things: the will of God and the plan of the Enemy.

As I have become more aware of the enemy's schemes, I'm not afraid, and I don't react in a panic. It's more like hearing a weather forecast of a storm coming. If I'm informed, I can prepare. The favor of God, then, isn't an easy life; it's a wise, powerful, God-honoring life.

Watchman Nee bursts some bubbles, changes expectations, and reorients our view of trouble when he writes, "When we meet suffering we then learn obedience. Such obedience is real. Our usefulness is not determined by whether or not we have suffered, but how much obedience we have learned through suffering. The obedient ones alone are useful to God."[11]

If the Lord is whispering to you to start this kind of prayer group, you may not have all the answers yet, but start somewhere. Gather your staff or your board or a small group of people whose walk with Christ you trust, and pray for an hour a week. Share your vision for the power of prayer in your church, ask God for wisdom to chart a course and build a fireplace, and trust the Spirit to send the fire. He will.

As time goes on, the Lord will put others on your heart to invite, and a few may decide that deeper levels of spiritual vulnerability and commitment aren't for them. Let them go without a hint of criticism. They may come back with more zeal than you can imagine.

Above all, listen to the voice of God and obey Him.

THINK ABOUT IT . . .

1. What is your understanding and experience of listening to the voice of God?

2. What elements of the principles and practice seem good and right to you? Which ones seem beyond what you believe God wants to do?

3. Who are some mature, spiritual, committed people who would be interested in this kind of weekly prayer? When and how will you begin?

CHAPTER 11

FREEDOM QUEST

One of the most frustrating things for me—and for many other pastors—is to pray with people at the altar who want to give their lives to Jesus, only to see them continue in destructive habits and remain in bondage to sin. When people get saved at our church, we realize it's the first step in a long process of spiritual growth. We invite them to a new believers' class, and we encourage them to join a small group. But even then, many people continue to struggle because of the recurring sins and the strongholds in their minds. We needed to find a better way to help them break free so they could grow.

We were determined to rethink our assimilation process for new Christians. They didn't just need biblical training on prayer and tithing; they needed to be set free. In other words, we needed to help them clear the stage of their hearts so their spiritual lives could be built on a solid, uncluttered foundation. Discipleship has to start with clearing away the debris of the past before people can effectively learn new habits for their future. To accomplish this objective, we created Freedom Quest, an event designed to address the prevailing sins, the false beliefs, and the pervasive doubts that form piles of spiritual, emotional, and relational rubble preventing personal progress.

Many people in our churches are, to one degree or another, still in bondage to habitual sins. Their sins have been forgiven by the blood of Christ, they've experienced the new birth, and they've had encounters with the Spirit of God, but they still struggle with some of the same sins they brought into their new lives. They want to be set free, but no one has shown them how—and perhaps, no one has even told them it's possible! Jesus told the woman caught in adultery, "Go and sin no more" (John 8:11, NKJV). Jesus' teaching is crystal clear. He knew that people were woefully enslaved to sin, yet He proclaimed, "If the Son makes you free, you shall be free indeed" (John 8:36). As Charles Wesley beautifully wrote, Jesus "breaks the power of cancelled sin and sets the captive free."[12]

Flowers don't grow in concrete, and spiritual sons and daughters don't thrive in the shallow soil of past wounds, experiences of abuse or addiction, strongholds, habitual sins, or a single sin so bad it still haunts them. God wants to set them free to know Him, love Him, and serve Him!

ME FIRST

Before starting Freedom Quest, I had heard about the powerful impact such twenty-four-hour events had on people, but I made a rookie mistake: I thought I could lead one without having participated in one. Dumb . . . really dumb.

I met with a spiritual, prophetic counselor who asked me really hard questions about my past behavior, my relationships, my defense mechanisms, and my secret thoughts—and then he asked even deeper questions. The process was painful and awkward, but absolutely necessary. I realized that I hadn't addressed all those things for two reasons: I hadn't realized many of them even existed, and I was ashamed of the ones I knew about. Both of those reasons kept me in the dark . . . and in a degree of bondage.

My counselor helped me acknowledge a lot of hidden sins and addictive behaviors that I had more or less successfully managed my entire life but hadn't destroyed and replaced. Confession (agreeing with God about our sin and His forgiveness) and repentance (to change one's mind; the decision to turn from sin to God and obedience) aren't just theological words; they form the path to a new and vibrant life of freedom. I was finally ready to help others find freedom, too.

OUR QUEST

Let me sketch the elements of our Freedom Quest:

Preparation

On Wednesday night we have a "Carpe Diem Lesson" to get everyone prepared for a life-changing weekend. We talk about the purpose of the Freedom Quest to instill excitement and hope that God will do something wonderful in their lives. We pair the participants with their mentors; and we hand out Spiritual Profiles that will expose many things for them to talk and pray about with their mentors.

Mentors

Weeks before the event, mentors are carefully screened and trained. They are the linchpins of success. Incredible things inevitably happen if the mentors make meaningful connections with their partners; if they don't, the diminished results are evident. Our team leaders spend time praying about the pairings and listening for God to direct us.

Our team leaders spend time praying about the pairings and listening for God to direct us.

Curriculum

The Freedom Quest begins on Friday at 5 p.m. and concludes at 5 p.m. on Saturday. The topics we cover include:

- A Look Back (The past doesn't determine the future)
- Condemnation vs. Justification (The cross of Christ forgives, cleanses, and sets us free)
- Life in the Spirit vs. Life in the Flesh (Dead Man Walking; Luke 9:23 and Romans 8)
- Taking Thoughts Captive (The lies of the Enemy)
- Identity: Owning Who We Are (Replacing wrong sources of identity with our identity in Christ)
- The Root Spirits (Overcoming spiritual strongholds)
- How We Allow the Enemy in Our Lives (Recognizing and defeating Satan's schemes to use sin, fear, and doubt)
- The Road Ahead (Next steps of growth)

FIRST STEPS

As soon as the Freedom Quest ends, we invite the participants to leave the hotel and drive over to our Core prayer meeting that starts at 6 p.m. We tell them, "When you walk into the room with these people who are praying, it will be one of the most powerful experiences of your life. In the last twenty-four hours, you've done business with God. You've had insights, you've confessed and repented, and you've grieved long-buried hurts. You've never been as clean and free as you are at this moment. The people already in the room are red hot in their passion for God. All week, they've been praying for God to use this weekend to set you free and give you a deep desire to please Him. When we go in, I'm going to teach you how to receive the baptism in the Holy Spirit. Are you ready?"

Yes, they're ready! It's a glorious and powerful time. After this meeting, each mentor invites the attendee to continue his or her Freedom Quest for the next twelve weeks (see below) to ensure a strong foundation in biblical truth, consolidate spiritual gains, and deal with additional strongholds, wounds, and sins that will inevitably surface. After the twelve weeks, we have a very good idea which people are serious about walking with God in the power of the Spirit, and which ones experienced a brief upsurge at the Freedom Quest that, for some reason, didn't take root.

If your church doesn't have a Core prayer meeting on Saturday nights, this sequence of events won't work. In that case I encourage you to have a session on the baptism in the Spirit near the end of your Freedom Quest. Then invite people who attended to come to your prayer meeting whenever the next one is scheduled.

TESTIMONIES AND DEMONSTRATIONS

On Sunday morning after the Freedom Quest, we provide an opportunity for people to share publicly what God has been doing in their lives. Some feel comfortable verbalizing their testimony of the last twenty-four hours, but many either aren't verbal communicators or can't yet put their experience into words. As an alternative, we provide a table of craft items: colored construction paper, glue, pipe cleaners, feathers, scissors, and all kinds of other things. We ask people to make a creative, visible representation of the impact of the Freedom Quest weekend on their lives, then we give them a short time in the Sunday morning service to talk about the craft they created. Because we have multiple Sunday morning services, we record their testimonials and share them over the upcoming weeks in services and on our website.

After everyone has had a chance to share their crafts, I quote a passage from Revelation 12:11: "They triumphed over [the enemy] by the blood of the Lamb and by the word of their testimony." I encourage them, "Now go and tell your friends what God has done for you."

FOLLOW-UP

The twenty-four hours of the Freedom Quest is incredibly powerful, but it shouldn't remain an isolated event. People have been set free, and now they need to learn how to live in their newfound freedom and power. The curriculum we've developed for the twelve weeks is comprised of basic discipleship principles, plus the additional element of the practice of uncovering wounds to be healed and sins to be forgiven. The process begins at the Freedom Quest, but all of us have more junk in our lives than can be effectively resolved in a single day.

The mentor who shepherded the person during the Freedom Quest takes him or her through the twelve additional weeks of teaching, prayer, repentance, and direction. This, of course, is a significant commitment for both people, and it's one that usually forms lifelong friendships. The mentor is the only one who knows the person's deepest hurts, fears, and sins. Confidentiality is assured, with the exception of cases of homicidal or suicidal ideation, or child or elder abuse. None of this is a surprise to the participants. We make it crystal clear to them at the beginning of the Freedom Quest.

The twelve weeks are designed to help people develop and internalize new habits of faithfulness to God. We don't take shortcuts. We keep up with the mentors to see who may need additional help along the way. Even at the end of the twelve weeks, it's not really over. The person who has completed this process is now ready for more responsibility in the kingdom. We consider inviting them to the School of Supernatural Ministry or to be mentors in the next Freedom Quest and twelve weeks of discipleship.

With each cycle, love and leadership multiply. As God clears the stage in every area of church life, more people are touched, more people are empowered and enthused with the Spirit of God, and more people hear the voice of God and respond to Him in glad obedience.

MORE THAN A PROGRAM

You don't have to use our model for Freedom Quest. You can adopt it, adapt it, or create your own. Whatever plan you use, go through the process yourself before you lead a weekend for your people. Realize this is much more than a program. If it's only a program to plug into your church calendar, please don't do it. Freedom Quest, like the Core, is part of a comprehensive work of the Spirit to infuse people with more spiritual awareness, love, and power than they (or you) ever imagined. The concepts and practices in the twenty-four hours of the Freedom Quest and the twelve-week curriculum are good and solid Bible content, but they need to be empowered by the work of the Spirit to be as effective as God intends for them to be. Settle for nothing less. Pray persistently and passionately.

But it all must begin with you. No matter how long it takes, find a mentor who will push you, pull you, encourage you, and challenge you to do business with God. To the extent you experience the freedom and power of the Spirit, you can teach, model, and impart freedom and power to your people. It's our responsibility to pastor our people through this process. Only when the Holy Spirit has gripped your heart should you consider implementing any of the models in this section of the book. To implement the program without personal preparation is like handing a machine gun to a three-year-old. It's foolish, irresponsible, and dangerous. The gun is effective and useful only in the hands of a trained and skilled warrior.

To the extent you experience the freedom and power of the Spirit, you can teach, model, and impart freedom and power to your people.

It's always important to select, train, and place mentors with the right participants. It will come as no surprise that my advice is to pray diligently about your mentors. Ask God to show you the people to select, how to equip them, and the participants to place each mentor with for the day and the twelve weeks. The quality of these relationships is crucial. Don't take them for granted, and don't make assumptions.

Listen to the Lord. It's a certainty that He'll lead you to make connections you would never have made on your own. Perhaps months later, you'll see why.

Providing a safe place for people to experience spiritual breakthroughs can become a normal part of your church's life. We have Freedom Quests twice a year. When Scott heard about it, he asked me to lead one for the leaders of The Oaks. His staff, his board members, and other top leaders of his church found a freedom they never knew existed.

In one of the last sessions together, we asked people to come up to share what God had done in their lives. One of the people who spoke was Clayton Brooks, the worship pastor at The Oaks. Here's what he said to us:

> I've been a worship leader at The Oaks for over fifteen years. Within that time, I've learned a great deal about music, teamwork, and leadership. I've been blessed with some truly exemplary and godly pastors who have faithfully modeled and taught me how to be a powerful leader in the kingdom of God. I'm also privileged to have grown up with the blessings of a Christ-centered family. God has been working deep in my heart to help me understand one of my most vital and challenging responsibilities as a man of God.
>
> It all began with an impromptu meeting with my pastor, Scott. For a year prior to this meeting, he had

been on quite an amazing journey with God. I thank the Lord for a senior pastor who cares so much about the people that, as he grows in the Lord, he openly shares what he's learning. I'm one of the beneficiaries of that kind of leadership, and God used him to begin dismantling the walls of fear and insecurity in my heart.

On a Tuesday morning after an all-staff meeting, Pastor Scott sat down with me and my music and vocal directors. He told us, "I appreciate you guys and all that you do for the people of The Oaks. You and your team are a blessing to this house. I love and appreciate the sweetness and humility with which you lead worship every week. But right now, we're not on the same page. This is such a pivotal season for our church, and I'm feeling the weight of teaching and pastoring everyone to be obedient to the leading of the Spirit . . . but I can only do so much on my own. Clayton, you've been given almost the same amount of on-stage leadership in this church as I have. You're responsible for almost half of the time scheduled in our weekend services. And I'm telling you right now . . . you have to grow! I and the rest of this church need you to step into the authority and boldness that God has given you as a leader in this house!"

It's hard to list all the thoughts that were running through my head as I listened to Scott speak.

I've been at The Oaks since I was a ten-year-old boy, and since I've been here, he has been my pastor. I'm a product of his leadership. I can remember when he was our youth pastor. He would preach and teach with such passion. This is a man who truly pours out his heart for the growth and benefit of other people. He has meant the world to me and to my development as a leader. As you can imagine, the things he said to me at that moment carried a *ton* of weight, and he was right on. I was sitting there recounting all the challenges God had already been putting in my heart over the last year, but for some reason, I hadn't been fully responding to the Spirit. It was quite clear that there was an obstacle in the way, and I knew exactly what it was.

My music and vocal directors shared with Pastor Scott that they were in agreement. We all wanted to be on the same page, but I knew I needed to do something a little deeper, because what was holding these things back in my heart had deep roots. I asked Pastor Scott if I could talk with him alone, and the other two guys left the room.

I told him, "Pastor Scott, I've been at this church since I was a ten-year-old boy, and you have been my pastor all of these years. You've been such a powerful influence on my life, and I'm beyond thankful for what your leadership has meant to me. But I have to be honest. I agree wholeheartedly with what you are saying. I want to be the bold and authoritative leader that God has called me to be for this house. And I can see how that can make a difference for you and the church. But something is holding me back. I'm scared . . . scared of disappointing you . . . scared of making mistakes that would mislead people and hurt what you're trying to do as our pastor. You and I both know that we are very different people. You've always been such a powerful and inspiring leader—so passionate and vocal about your love for the Lord and your desire to help people grow. I've always been a quiet one—happy to be one of the followers down the line and uncomfortable in positions of authority. I almost find it funny that God has seen fit to have me in this position. I know I can perform well, but this fear causes me to keep confined to what I know I can do as a worship leader. I'm hiding behind what I know I can do and what's safe. And honestly, I can hear God in you saying that it's time to grow. I've been hearing Him say that over the past year. I just don't know if it's possible—or maybe it's that it's just not going to be possible here."

My voice shook as I said these things. It's hard to share weaknesses with others. It's *very* hard to share weaknesses with people you admire dearly. But it *had* to happen. He and I both knew that something needed to change. A person can't grow without changing.

After a pause, Pastor Scott responded to me, "Clayton, I love you, and I appreciate your desire to be submitted to me as your pastor. But it sounds to me that you're more concerned about disappointing *me* than you are about disappointing *God*. And when it comes to making mistakes . . . Clayton, you are *so far* from making mistakes. I would actually prefer, as your pastor, that you make some mistakes! Then we can fix them and learn from them. But right now, you're allowing the fear of people to dictate your obedience to God. And that fear has locked up your potential, and potentially, what God wants to do for The Oaks."

I said to him, "Well, I know God has been telling me to grow."

He quickly replied, "He's been *shouting* it, Clayton! And, you know what? I'm your pastor. I love you, and I want you here. But more than that, I desperately want you to be able to grow in the Lord. And if that means you buck up and grow here, or if that means you have to go somewhere else, I'll support you. *But you cannot stay the same anymore!*"

There was another pause in our conversation as all of this was sinking deep into my heart. Those words resounded with every heartbeat: "You cannot stay the same. You cannot stay the same. You cannot stay the same." I was beginning to get a very real understanding of what God was doing.

I looked at my pastor tearfully. "What would you do?" I asked.

"If I were you? I would get in my prayer closet, repent of having a greater desire to please people than God, and tell God that you want to change and start living in complete obedience to Him. That's what I would do. As soon as possible."

With that I told him, "Thank you," and did exactly what he said.

I walked up to a room that's hidden away in our church. It's a place that I sometimes go to pray. I began to wrestle with the Lord about all of this.

"God . . . I'm scared. I'm not quite sure what all of this is going to mean, and it scares me! I'm nervous that I'm going to look foolish in front of others. I'm afraid You're going to have me do something and my fears will mess it all up. I'm not good enough for You. I have nothing to offer!"

With that, I began to do "the ugly cry." It was one of those cries where your mouth is wide open, but you can't make any noise come out. It hurt. Evidently, over the years, a lot of walls of fear had built up throughout my life.

I was reminded of a counseling session my wife and I had a couple of years into our marriage. In our second session with the counselor, he looked at me and said, "You're powerful!" It was something he knew I didn't really believe, but something he knew I needed to start believing. At that moment the only thought going through my mind was how weak and afraid I was.

Now, at this moment, in this prayer time up in a tucked-away room at The Oaks, all of my weaknesses were appearing before me. I knew that God was calling me to be completely obedient to Him, and I knew that meant I would have to surrender my pride, my comfort, my self-preservation, and that God was going to have me practice that obedience in the near future.

When I said I had nothing to offer, I first felt like I heard God speak. He said to me, "You're right. You have nothing to offer this world and this church. Apart from Me you can do nothing. It's in realizing your humanity that you begin to understand your dependence on Me. And that is right where I want you: dependent on Me."

Then God told me something I didn't want to hear at all: "Clayton, I want you to be a prophet."

I reacted, "Please, God. I don't want to be a prophet! Prophets are weird. Please don't do that to me!"

"They're not weird," He assured me. "They are willing to obey Me without hesitation, to trust My commands no matter who it might offend or disappoint. And *that* is what I want from you."

I replied, "Lord, You heard what my pastor said, and he's right. I'm all locked up! Even if I wanted to say yes to You, I wouldn't know what to do! How am I supposed to do what You're asking me to do when my spirit is all locked up by fear? What can I do?"

And God shouted, *"I gave you a key!"*

To explain this comment, let me take you back to a moment ten years earlier. I was leading worship for our youth group at a retreat. Our speaker that weekend was Edwin Ennis, who has had a longtime connection with The Oaks. During the last session, he stopped his message and began to give prophetic words to different students and leaders in the audience. He called my name, and I stood up. He walked up to me and put something in my hand. It was an old key. He said, "I don't know where this key came from, and what it unlocks, but God told me to give this to you. One day you're going to be where the door in front of you is locked, and it's a door you'll know you need to go through. You won't know what to do, but God is saying, 'I'm giving you the key for when that time comes.'"

Ten years later, I still had that key. It was in my bag in that prayer room with me. And when God shouted, *"I gave you a key!"* I pulled it out of the side pocket of my bag. As I clutched the key tightly in my hand, I began to feel hopeful—maybe it really *was* possible for me to be a prophet and completely obedient to God without fear.

From that point, God took the better part of an hour to speak to me and surround me with His loving presence. It happened that in the weekend coming up, the leadership of our church was having a Freedom Quest that I planned to attend. God confirmed that this was His timing and spoke into my spirit that something special would happen at this retreat, but it would require my complete obedience. I answered, "Yes, Lord."

The retreat began that Friday night. During one of the prayer times, the men from FFI who were guiding us through the retreat were asked to give a word of encouragement to each of us who attended. An older man I didn't know approached me and said, "Trust in the Lord with all your heart and lean not on your own understanding." This resonated greatly in me, because I knew God was going to ask me to do something—but I didn't know when, what, and if it would even make sense.

We had a great evening that Friday. Saturday morning, one of the pastors from the other church invited us to share what God had been speaking to us so far at the retreat. After a few men shared, I felt like I was supposed to tell everyone in the room that God wanted me to do something special, but it would come later. Right then wasn't the time. I made this announcement as a commitment and a promise that I'd follow through. Later, after a wonderful time of worship with the men, the pastor asked if it was the right time, and I felt it was.

In the room were forty men from The Oaks. They were elders, directors, and staff pastors—including Pastor Scott and my dad. Also in the room were all the men from the other church who served as mentors at the Freedom Quest. I walked to the center of the room, still not completely sure what I was going to do.

I told the men that everything I was about to do was in strict obedience to the Lord. He was giving me the opportunity to obey His commands. I took my rings and my glasses off, and I set them on the table behind me. I pulled my shoes off, and then I asked my dad to come join me. Then I spoke to him so everyone could hear: "Dad, I love you with all my heart. I'm so thankful for you and all you have done for me. I have the utmost respect for you, and I am submitted to you. *But I am the Lord's,* and He is calling me out as His own."

Then I asked Pastor Scott to come forward and stand next to my dad, and I spoke to him: "Pastor Scott, you are my pastor. I love you, and I thank you for all you've done for me and taught me. I'm submitted to you and your God-given vision for our church. *But I am the Lord's,* and He is calling me out as His own."

Then I spoke to the men of The Oaks. I apologized for all the opportunities for spiritual breakthrough in our services that never happened because I was simply too afraid to step out in faith and obedience. I told them that God was calling me out as His own, to be a prophet—completely obedient to Him. I could no longer be afraid. I had to obey the Lord, no matter how foolish it made me feel.

As the Lord led me, I messed up my hair in front of all of them—no glasses, no rings, no shoes, and a messy head of hair. Then I said to the Lord, "It's just You and me now." I then began to speak in tongues, which I had never done publicly. And I wasn't merely speaking. I could sense the power of the Lord in me causing me to proclaim the expression in tongues, loudly and passionately. I began to prophesy and interpret the message, lifting up praise to God.

For the next five minutes, it seemed like the whole room full of men was erupting with spontaneous praise. I saw men on the floor, I heard them shouting and praising, and I saw them lifting their hands to God. It was such a powerful moment of breakthrough. The Lord was in it! As it quieted down, I made my way back to my seat, and John Bates said, "Do you see what God does in response to an act of complete obedience?" It was a life-changing moment for me, but I knew that one other person needed to be up there with my dad and my pastor, and that was my wife, Aunie.

When I arrived home that night, Aunie and I put the kids to bed, and then we talked about the retreat. I told her that before I could talk about what the Lord had done in me, I needed to do something. I had her stand up in front of me just like my dad and Pastor Scott did. I went through the same process in front of her that the Lord had me go through at the retreat. I had never spoken in tongues quite like that in front of my wife. After I had spoken in tongues, God began to give me prophetic words to speak over her, our boys, our home, and myself. It was such a beautiful moment of breakthrough for me and for us, and I will never forget it.

The following day was Sunday, and I knew that Pastor Scott was going to have me share what was going on in my life. I took the people of The Oaks through the process. By this time, the Lord had revealed to me what everything meant, so I explained it to them.

I took off my shoes, because my identity and self-worth is not found in where I am or what I do for a living. I took off my rings, because my identity and self-worth is not found in my relationships—even those that mean the most to me, like my marriage, and with my dad and my pastor. I took off my glasses, because my identity is not found in the affirming or disappointed looks on people's faces when they encounter me. And I messed up my hair, because my value is not found in my appearance. Then the Lord had me speak in tongues and prophesy before the whole church. The public expression of tongues was the ultimate proof for me that I could respond to the Lord's leading, even if it doesn't make sense—and that I could do it as a leader in front of other people. The people began to come to the altar and passionately seek the Lord. It was a very powerful morning of breakthrough at The Oaks.

Through this experience, God gave me a new sense of security in Him—so much that I was able to stand in front of a crowd of people, including those whose opinions I've always valued the most, and

> simply be God's man. I still fight feelings of insecurity, but the Lord has done a miraculous work in me. His grace is sufficient and makes all the difference.

We asked Clayton to tell how the experience has shaped his life since the Freedom Quest. He told us,

> Since this event, God has empowered me to flow in more authority and prophetic anointing than I've ever experienced. My relationship with the Lord has become much more disciplined. My wife and I pray together on a regular basis, and my team and I pray over every detail of our planning for worship ministry. New songs, prophetic songs and prayers, have been pouring out of my heart and the hearts of those on my team—songs that our church is beginning to sing and pray. God's voice is being magnified through the work He's done in the leaders of our church!
>
> And I'm at rest. There's a wonderful rest people find when they discover that all the Lord requires is to be obedient to Him. I don't need to impress anyone. I don't even need people to respond affirmatively to my leadership. Like the prophets of old who obeyed God and spoke His word even when people hated them, all I need to be is obedient. That's all, and that's enough. In that simplicity is a wonderful rest. The pressure of being amazing and impressive

is no longer there, only the pressure to obey God's commands. I realized that if we seek His commands, we will find them in *every* situation. He *loves* it when we want to partner with Him to do His work.

Spiritual leaders have the authority to call out greatness from their followers. God has given such responsibility to act upon, even if it risks losing some. It has meant so much to me that my pastor would trust me to authoritatively lead the worship in our church every weekend. It has also meant a great deal that he would care more about my personal growth in the Lord than my effectiveness as a worship leader in his church. He has exemplified a new depth of trust in the Lord and a new level of pastoral leadership.

Worship leaders, you have almost as much face time in front of your church as your senior pastor. What a great responsibility God has entrusted to you! Don't be scared of disappointing people. Be submissive to your pastoral authority, but keep God first! Allow Him the opportunity to use you to inspire others! Let the Spirit of God inform all of your decision-making. Stay submitted to your pastor for as long as you are under his authority, but don't sacrifice the leading of the Spirit for anything. You'll make some mistakes, but you'll learn and grow—and you, your pastor, your family, and your church will be blessed and strengthened by your obedience to the Lord.

One of the miracles of grace is that God is willing to turn our pain into compassion and our sins into stepping-stones of growth. Our new freedom doesn't mean we don't remember the heartaches and foolish decisions we've made. Instead, we marvel that God weaves even our tragedies and worst sins into a beautiful new tapestry of His glory . . . if we'll trust Him. Then we can use the lessons we've learned to care for others who are struggling to be free. As they experience God's love and power, their hurts are healed, they overcome a lifetime of bondage, and they are ready to help even more people find new freedom in Christ.

THINK ABOUT IT . . .

1. Think carefully about your current spiritual condition. Don't rush your analysis. Get into your prayer closet and ask yourself, "Am I truly free?" Ask your heavenly Father to reveal any areas of bondage you still experience, and ask Him to set you free. Journal your reflection and prayers.

2. What portions of the Freedom Quest seem easy to plan? What parts require more of you than you've ever given before?

3. How would you describe the role of mentors in this event? Why are the three months of follow-up meetings essential?

4. What would you ask or say to Clayton if he were with you right now?

CHAPTER 12

THE SCHOOL OF SUPERNATURAL MINISTRY

Before I learned to operate in the prophetic, I was a pastor on autopilot. Every week I went through the same routine of planning services, sermons, and programs. I said I was doing things *for* God, but I certainly wasn't doing those things *with* God. I operated out of my ideas, my plans, and my strength.

When I encountered God, He gave me a hunger for the prophetic word. I began reading books by pastors who effectively and wisely used the gifts. I also read Acts and was confused that the things God did in the early church didn't seem to be happening—as much or in the same way—as I read in those pages. I had grown up in churches where tongues, interpretation, and healing were common, but not words of prophecy, knowledge, or wisdom. Leaders in those churches were afraid of the excesses of some pastors who claimed their prophetic words were equal to Scripture. But avoiding those gifts, I began to understand, wasn't a healthy response to that problem.

I realized how much I had shortchanged the people in our church, so one Sunday I confessed to them that I had been doing church without God. I explained that it had never been my intention to be rebellious and hardhearted. I hadn't understood the spiritual dynamic of the Spirit and the gifts, but now I was ready to learn. I told them I had suffered from my ignorance, and because of my leadership in this area, they had suffered.

UNINFORMED

As Paul began a lengthy explanation for the Corinthians of the role of spiritual gifts in the church, he told them, "Now about the gifts of the Spirit, brothers and sisters, I do not want you to be uninformed" (1 Cor. 12:1). Uninformed. That was my condition as a pastor, and that's exactly the condition of many believers regarding the gifts of the Spirit. They are ignorant, in the dark, misinformed, unlearned, and out to lunch. In chapters 12–14 of 1 Corinthians, he attempts to make them informed, knowledgeable, intelligent, learned, and enlightened. That's my goal, too. The symbol we use for our church is a light bulb. It represents the light of God's truth as well as the fact that the light of God overpowers the darkness in our lives.

At FFI, we teach people about all the gifts found in the four major lists: Romans 12, 1 Corinthians 12, Ephesians 4, and 1 Peter 4. In our School of Supernatural Ministry, we bring a clear focus to the nine "sign gifts" in 1 Corinthians. Since Paul said the chief among these is prophecy, I wanted to camp on this gift first.

Gradually, carefully, I began inserting teaching about the prophetic gifts into my sermons, my prayer gatherings, and into my conversations. For instance, I sometimes prayed, "Lord, show each of us something we've never seen before—about Your love and power, about Your will for us, or about something in us needing to change." I asked people to let me know if God had spoken to them. And quite often, He did.

I told our people to write down their dreams in the morning and ask God, "Was this a result of the pizza I ate last night, or were You speaking to me?"

Sometimes in our services I sense God is speaking to people in the room. I stop and say, "We often think visions and words of prophecy are strange, but some of you just had one. If you did, tell the person sitting next to you that God just spoke to you or showed you something." Gradually, people are learning to expect God to speak to them in a still, small voice, in dreams and visions, and through prophetic words from others. Our congregation is a laboratory for all of us to try out what we are learning.

To help people understand how God might speak to them, I told our congregation, "Close your eyes and imagine you have a knife and a lemon. Now imagine holding the lemon in one hand and cutting it with the knife. Feel the skin and the pressure of the knife. Smell the juice as drops fall on the counter." I gave them a few seconds, and then I said, "Open your eyes. Did you feel it? Did you almost smell it? That's the sense of reality we have when God speaks to us in supernatural ways. It's beyond our normal thinking and imagination." The psalmist encouraged us to, "Taste and see that the LORD is good" (Ps. 34:8). As we seek God, He lets us taste, see, and feel His presence.

FIRST ATTEMPTS

I knew the Lord wanted to give me words of prophecy for believers in our church. I asked God to reveal words to me and identify the people who would receive them, and He answered my prayers. I have to admit that I had a few pitfalls along the way. I was uninformed, and I made some mistakes. I didn't have the experience or wisdom to know that some words should be given in private instead of public.

One Sunday a number of visitors came to our church. At the end of the service several of them came forward. As they stood at the altar, God gave me a word for a particular lady. I assumed that if God gave it to me in the service, I should speak it in the service. Wrong. I should have gone to her privately and said, "I believe the Lord gave me a word for you this morning. If you would like to hear it, I'd like to speak with you privately. For propriety, I'll have another lady with me in our conversation. Would you like to talk with me?"

But instead, I announced for all to hear: "I have a word for you today. God has shown me a vision of you in a cage with eight bars. You've been in bondage, and God wants to set you free!"

I thought she would be thrilled and relieved. She smiled and nodded, but I could tell she was reserved.

The next day, she called to tell me she and her husband, a physician, had been in Assemblies of God churches all their lives, and she had never been so humiliated. She informed me that she and her husband were never coming back. She didn't stop there. She gave me a piece of advice I've never forgotten: "Pastor, you need to stop publicly humiliating people. It's offensive, and it's crazy!"

I got the message. I was devastated. I apologized to her, and I told the Lord, "Oh my, I really missed it."

I told the leaders of our church about the lady's response, and I explained that I needed to take a break from the prophetic for a while to learn how to do it more compassionately and effectively. I needed training. God wanted to clear

God wanted to clear the stage of anything in my ministry that was cluttered by my uninformed way of ministering in these gifts.

the stage of anything in my ministry that was cluttered by my uninformed way of ministering in these gifts.

Not long after that experience, I drove to a meeting with a leader in our fellowship. On the way as I prayed, the Lord told me, "He is going to correct you. Listen to him. Don't be afraid . . . receive it." Immediately, I thought of a dozen things he might feel the need to correct in my life and ministry.

Our meeting lasted about two hours. It was very productive, but he hadn't said any words of correction. Before I got up, I said, "On the way here, the Lord told me you had some words of correction for me. I'm ready to listen."

He smiled, opened his desk drawer, and pulled out a letter. He said, "Yes, I was going to show you this letter from a doctor's wife who attended your church. She was upset with you, but I'm sure you already knew that." I nodded. He continued, "But in our meeting today, you've shown me you're on track with God. You've learned the lessons God wanted to teach you about using the prophetic word in your church. I don't need to correct you. God has already done that. You hear from God, so go and prophesy. Don't be afraid." What an affirmation for my aching pastoral soul! I knew like never before that God wanted me to continue to learn and grow.

EQUIPPING THE SAINTS

The reason I started a School of Supernatural Ministry at our church is that this is a marketplace ministry, and everybody gets a flame. I didn't want a business leader to get a word from the Lord about an employee or boss and make a dramatic—and inappropriate—pronouncement in front of a room of peers.

For a while, I was "the prophecy hog." I was virtually the only one receiving words of prophecy, wisdom, and knowledge from the Lord. But my role is to equip the saints for the work of ministry. I had to inform, teach, train, and model the use of the gifts so others would become proficient. Let me share a few operating principles:

Invitations

I invite specific people to attend our School of Supernatural Ministry, and of course, we focus on knowing, hearing, and obeying the voice of God. We teach this simple but profound truth to every age and group in our church, from the youngest children to our pastoral staff. It's important for a pastor to clear the stage to provide the right environment for everyone to live in a new day in the Spirit.

We meet from 5 p.m. to 6 p.m. on Saturdays, right before the Core prayer meeting. I usually teach for about forty minutes, and then we have an exercise and practice for the rest of the time.

Everyone

I believe all nine of the sign gifts in 1 Corinthians 12 are available to every believer, but some people have an elevated, God-inspired ability to operate in one or more of these gifts. It's like all the rest of the gifts: Everyone serves, but some have the spiritual gift of service. Everyone should be a witness, but some have the gift of evangelism. Everybody gives, but God has given some the ability to make a lot of money and the wisdom to give it strategically for the kingdom. This principle is true for all the gifts.

The nine gifts

All of the charismata are given to believers for the purpose of building up and enlarging the body of Christ. These spiritual gifts are, for this reason, antithetical to our selfish human nature. We naturally want applause and power, but the gifts only function appropriately when we use them to glorify God and care for others. They're about Christ's reputation, not ours. They're about the needs of others, not our wants. Christopher Wright explains, "Anointing by the Spirit is not primarily an external thing that proves its presence by noise (though of course the Spirit of God can make a great deal of noise on occasion, as on the day of Pentecost). Rather, spiritual anointing is primarily an equipping for mission, a commissioning for service."[13]

In the School of Supernatural Ministry we train people to operate in all nine spiritual gifts Paul lists in 1 Corinthians 12:1–10. Different biblical scholars present the charismata in different categories of relationship. Don't let these differences create any confusion. The most important thing is that edification occurs, not how we categorize the gifts. At FFI we lay out these gifts in the following categories:

Revelatory gifts

Words of wisdom

Words of knowledge

Discerning of spirits

Vocal gifts

Prophecy

Speaking in tongues

Interpretation of tongues

Power gifts

Faith

Healing

Working of miracles

A gift for many

Paul told the Corinthians three times that they should eagerly desire the gifts (1 Cor. 12:31; 14:1, 39). Dr. Paul Brooks writes that this desire "should be understood not merely as a desire to witness or hear the gifts in action but a desire to engage as participants."[14] The apostle Paul especially highlighted prophecy in two of the three references: "desire earnestly spiritual gifts, but especially that you may prophesy" (1 Cor. 14:1), and "desire earnestly to prophesy" (1 Cor. 14:39). As we've seen, this gift is for encouraging, strengthening, and comforting the people of God

(1 Cor. 14:3). I train our people to ask God for a word serving these purposes. If we think of someone and a thought comes to mind to encourage, strengthen, or comfort, we can be sure it's not from the Devil! The Spirit of God prompts our spirit to share encouraging words.

We don't need to stand back, roll up our sleeves, and loudly pronounce, "Thus saith the Lord!" We can simply say, "Hey, I was thinking about you and praying for you, and I sense the Lord has given me something to share with you. Would you mind if I tell you?" If the person doesn't respond as fertile soil prepared by God to receive our message, we know at least we spoke words of encouragement—and everybody needs those.

Why does Paul say, "especially that you may prophesy"? Clearly, he believes this is a gift that should function pervasively among the people. It's something of a "breakout gift" to move people forward into loving others through spiritual gifts. He goes on to say, "For you can all prophesy in turn so that everyone may be instructed and encouraged" (1 Cor. 14:31).

Let me ask you this: how many people who come to our churches each week need a word of encouragement, strength, or comfort—or all three? Virtually everybody! So it shouldn't be rare or surprising when the Spirit of God uses the people of God to share His heart through a prophetic word from God. It should be entirely normal. Can you encourage people? Then you can prophesy. Can you strengthen someone? Then you can prophesy. Can you provide comfort for a person who is hurting? Then you can prophesy. It's not some odd mystery reserved for a weird or super-spiritual few. It's for everybody. To do so, we need to be genuinely led by the Holy Spirit.

It shouldn't be rare or surprising when the Spirit of God uses the people of God to share His heart through a prophetic word from God.

All in love

When Paul explained the gifts to the Corinthians, he used three chapters (1 Cor. 12–14). The middle one is all about love. I call these three chapters "the love sandwich." It doesn't matter how flashy our gifts may be, how powerful our faith is, or how much we sacrifice for Christ's cause—if everything we do isn't done in love, it's utterly and completely worthless. There's just no sandwich without the meat. Likewise, love without the gifts isn't really love, because the acts of edification and other-centered service go unfulfilled. Too many leaders and believers have completely disconnected love and set it out on its own, but not Paul.

When we teach people about using the gifts, we remind them of this fact over and over again. Too often in the past, the sign gifts have been used as a power trip to impress people and earn prestige. That's not the spirit of love at all. Kindness, humility, gentleness, and patience are the hallmarks of authentic love. In *Surprised by the Voice of God*, Jack Deere observes succinctly, "The worst form of pride is religious pride."[15]

Practice

In our classes, we provide opportunities for our participants to practice. We put people in groups of three, and we give these instructions: One prays quietly in the Spirit. The second one asks God for a vision, a thought, or a word about the third person. The filter is this: "Is the message encouraging, strengthening, or comforting?" If it is, the second person shares it. The third person receives the word and gives feedback. After one person prophesies, the next person has a turn, and then the third. The feedback may be, "Wow, that spoke right to where I am right now!" Or it may be, "Thank you for praying for me." Either way, encouragement, strength, and comfort were imparted.

We sometimes get people into a circle, and I tell them to trust God for a word for the person next to them. I give them only a minute or two. This gives them experience of having a sense of immediacy in an encounter with someone. They can then use what they learn in any and every meeting with people throughout their day, even if it's only for a minute or two. In every moment, we can be sensitive to the Spirit and speak words of life.

Sometimes people who are learning how to use the gifts get off base. That's why we practice. No toddler is expected to run in an Olympic race. No person who is picking up a violin for the first time is expected to play like a virtuoso. In every aspect of life, there's a learning curve—it's the same in learning to practice the gifts.

Our school is a safe place to try and fail, a safe place to make mistakes, a safe place to learn new things, and a safe place to ask dumb questions. In fact, there are no dumb questions, just ones not yet answered.

Use questions

We've taught our people, and I've taught Scott, to ask questions for two reasons: to test to see if the word really fits the person, and to till the soil for a more responsive answer. When Scott was preaching one Sunday, he sensed God telling him that a young woman sitting near the front was having sex with her boyfriend, and she was struggling with guilt. The Lord told him to say to her, "You're my daughter, and I love you. I don't condemn you. Come to Me." During a time of prayer when things were quiet, Scott walked over to her and whispered, "How are you doing?"

She looked up and replied sadly, "Not that good."

He then asked, "How are things in your relationships?"

She looked surprised—exposed, but strangely glad to be known. She said, "What do you mean?"

Scott said, "Like with your boyfriend."

Now she looked shocked. "How did you know?"

Scott didn't tell her about the prophetic word. Instead, he asked, "Are things going well with you and your boyfriend? Are you honoring the Lord in all you do together?"

She began shaking her head and tears streamed down her face.

Scott told her gently, "The Lord told me to tell you, 'You're my daughter, and I love you. I don't condemn you. Come to Me.'" Some women in the church could tell she needed prayer, so they gathered around her and prayed for her. It was a beautiful and powerful moment in her life . . . and in Scott's.

As Scott has internalized these principles, he has been an incredible student, practitioner, and leader. I appreciate his heart, his courage, and his impact on the people in his church.

Convictions, or a word from God?

Some people confuse personal convictions with God-given prophetic words. They may feel strongly that someone ought to do this or that, but passion for their perspective isn't the same as knowing, hearing, and obeying God to relate a word from Him. Passionate people need a double filter on the things they care about most. When they feel the urge to correct someone, they need to stop, ask God to reveal their true motives, and proceed with a spirit of humility—determined to listen more than to speak. It would also be a good, long-term goal for all participants in the School of Ministry to identify their "hot buttons" so they can avoid confusing them with words from God.

Paul explained, "Now to each one the manifestation of the Spirit is given for the common good" (1 Cor. 12:7). The gifts aren't given to provide a platform for us to communicate our political ideology, our convictions about social ills, or any other hobbyhorse. It's for the benefit of others, not to make us feel more powerful and right.

The gifts aren't given to provide a platform for us to communicate our political ideology, our convictions about social ills, or any other hobbyhorse. It's for the benefit of others.

"Opposite day"

As people become more adept at perceiving and sharing prophetic words, they may notice signs of bondage, resistance, or sin in people. One of the most helpful principles we teach about prophetic words is to practice "opposite day." A person may walk into a room and the Spirit shows us he or she has a rebellious attitude. Instead of confronting the issue with an honest but harsh word, which usually results in even higher walls of resistance, we encourage the people we train to focus on the positive. Imagine what it would look like if the person responds to God's grace and truth. We might say to the rebel, "I can see the Lord is calling you to be sensitive and yielded to Him, and He wants to do great things in and through you. We're going to pray this over you today." That statement is absolutely the case, if the person repents. Instead of speaking judgment, we speak life and hope—the opposite of their current condition.

Final exams

At the end of each semester of our school, we have a test. I send people out two by two (a man with a man, a woman with a woman), and I tell them, "You have an hour to ask God for direction to lead you to someone who needs a prophetic word or a word of knowledge or wisdom, to work a miracle, or to pray for someone to be healed. I want you to go where God tells you to go, find who God tells you to find, and do the work God has given you to do. Come back in an hour and give a report."

We send them out into the neighborhoods and malls and shops. This isn't about staying in a safe place within the walls of the church. Jesus sent His disciples "to the lost sheep of Israel" as well as "to the ends of the earth." Our people can't get that far in an hour, but they can at least go a little way beyond their comfort zone.

Their "grade" isn't the "wow factor" of their word or miracle; it's the fact that they were obedient to do what God told them to do. Success is always in His hands, not ours.

Levels of experience and expertise

We've been teaching on these gifts for many years, so we have several tiers of classes for people, depending on their level of experience and comfort in using the gifts. I don't think we ever "master" the gifts, just as we never plumb the depths of God's infinite holiness, grace, love, and majesty.

SOONER OR LATER

Sometimes a prophetic word takes a long time to take root in our lives and bear fruit. This is not uncommon, so we should never quickly dismiss a prophetic word. Paul wrote, "Do not treat prophecies with contempt but test them all; hold on to what is good" (1 Thess. 5:20–21). Remember Clayton's story? A servant of God had prophesied over him and left him with a key. He carried that key in his bag for years. Then, at just at the right time, in the dark closet of his desperation, God met him with a glorious and liberating revelation.

Long before the Lord began giving me a hunger for the prophetic, and long before I switched off the autopilot as a pastor, God gave me a word. I was twenty years old, single, and a Bible college student. A man spoke at our chapel service. He also played the keyboard and led worship with his wife. He was giving very encouraging prophetic words to people. I felt a bit uncomfortable with it all. My heritage taught me to be wary of prophetic pronouncements . . . even positive ones.

A few days later, he spoke at a church nearby. A friend wanted to go, and he asked me to tag along. We sat in the back row. Sometime during the message, the man stopped and pointed to me. He said, "You came tonight to watch, but God has something for you. You were dedicated to ministry before you were born. God has a call on your life, and you'll have a ministry like mine. You'll prophesy, you'll marry a woman who sings, you'll play the keyboard, and you'll travel around the world doing healing crusades. God will use you to do great things in His kingdom." But he didn't stop there. There was a condition. He continued, "*If* you'll get over your crippling perfectionism. Just be you."

I'm not sure who was more surprised, my friend or me. Certainly, there was no hint of any of this in my life at the time.

I was angry . . . not at the guy or at God, but at my parents. They had never told me they dedicated me to ministry! I told them about the prophecy and asked why they hadn't told me. They just shrugged and said, "We knew you'd find out sooner or later."

Over the years, all of the man's words have come true, including my freedom from perfectionism. But being used by God took a long, long time. I was far too resistant, too set in my traditional ways, too unbelieving that the Spirit would work through me with grace and power.

In the past two decades, God has broken me, bent me, and reformed me. It has been both thrilling and grueling—it's been exactly what I needed to become the man God intended me to be. I've learned so much, but I feel like I'm only beginning to "know [the love of Christ] that surpasses knowledge" and to experience His "incomparably great power for us who believe" (Eph. 3:19; 1:19). The more I know, the more I realize how much I don't know. God is the only infallible, omniscient One. I'm just trying to know, listen, and obey moment by moment. I think He's pretty happy with that.

The strategy God has given us puts us in touch with the Spirit of God more fully and powerfully than anything I've ever experienced in leading a church, but it's only a strategy. You can adopt ours, adapt it, or create your own. It's not the form that matters; it's the heart. Ask God for a broken heart, an open heart, and a submissive heart—first for you and then for the people who will join you in creating a new culture in your church. Expect bumps along the way. We're fallen people living in a fallen world. The things of the Spirit of God are always bigger, deeper, and greater than we can imagine. We can't control them any more than we can get a grip on a hurricane. But the amazing force of the Spirit isn't destructive. He points us to the majesty of the Father and the tender, forgiving love of the Son. We are amazed that He would call us His own. Any strategy that is Spirit-led inevitably propels us toward more wonder, joy, and love than we ever dreamed possible.

THINK ABOUT IT . . .

1. Paul said three times, "Earnestly desire spiritual gifts!" Do you earnestly desire the gifts, and are you engaged in prayer about them? Write down your prayer to God about this.

2. How have you understood and experienced the nine gifts in 1 Corinthians 12?

3. What do you think has to happen to you before you can lead others in spiritual gifts?

4. When do you think you will be ready to conduct a School of Supernatural Ministry? What signs in your own life do you need to see? What signs do you need to see in the lives of those who want to attend?

5. What are your biggest hopes and biggest fears as you consider conducting this school?

CHAPTER 13

CULTURE SHIFT

Christ's kingdom is upside down to the way the world thinks and acts. It's radical, unnerving, unexpected, and actually, unwanted by many people who claim to follow Him. We would rather be happy than obedient. We'd rather be satisfied than hungry. Jesus said the way up is down, the last shall be first, the way to have true power is by choosing to become the lowest servant, the source of true riches is to give sacrificially, and the way to freedom is to admit we're slaves of sin.

Our American culture loves winners. In sports, business, the arts, and every other arena, winners are celebrated and losers forgotten. It's not much different in the church. Too often we glorify the winners, the leaders who have made it big, and we overlook the ones who faithfully serve Christ in obscurity.

If people are going to flow with the Spirit, we have to have a radical shift in our thinking, our values, and our culture. Everything in us, and everything in our leaders and followers, screams against this reorientation. But it's necessary. As always, it starts with you and me. If we aren't making progress in living according to the upside down principles of spiritual life, we can't expect others to do it either. We have to be first. Scott calls himself the "Lead Follower." That's a perfect example of a label describing the new culture, and we can't wait until people are on our leadership board before we communicate the upside-down kingdom. It has to be infused in every age group, every curriculum, every leadership meeting, every sermon, and every prayer. We take this new ground inch by inch.

BROKEN AND OPEN

Weakness . . . we avoid it like the plague. Vulnerability . . . we can't stand it so we cover up. Brokenness . . . we'd rather see ourselves as victors! One of the key components of the upside-down kingdom is that weakness is the open door to spiritual strength. The Beatitudes are an expression of this principle. The ones who are blessed are the poor in spirit, those who know in the depths of their souls they are bankrupt without God's grace. The blessed also include those who mourn, who are meek, who hunger and thirst for righteousness, who are merciful instead of intimidating, who seek peace instead of insisting on winning, and those who endure persecution for the sake of Christ (Matt. 5:3–12).

God doesn't leave theology in the books on our shelves. He brings His truth into our lives, often in the most inconvenient ways! Paul was taken into the third heaven and saw glories people don't usually see. He was tempted to be arrogant about his experience, but God brought him down with a "thorn in the flesh." Paul asked the Lord to remove it and give him relief, but God's agenda was different from the apostle's. The Lord assured him, "My grace is sufficient for you, for my power is made perfect in weakness." And Paul concluded,

> Therefore I will boast all the more gladly about my weaknesses, so that Christ's power may rest on me. That is why, for Christ's sake, I delight in weaknesses, in insults, in hardships, in persecutions, in difficulties. For when I am weak, then I am strong. (2 Cor. 12:9–10)

Delight in suffering? Can Paul be serious? Yes, but only because he was committed to an upside-down kingdom and a Spirit-enriched culture. All of us can have our own list of weaknesses and heartaches we have avoided, minimized, excused, rationalized, or hidden even from those who love us most. Here's a list that might ring a few bells:

- Gossip
- Exaggerating the truth, or blatant lies
- Angling for attention, admiration, and applause

- Living with a spirit of self-pity, resentment, and entitlement
- Ignoring the needs of others
- Empty religious activity
- Daydreaming about success, pleasure, or approval
- Structuring our lives to pursue success, pleasure, or approval more than God's kingdom
- Living under a cloud of doubts about God's greatness and grace
- Complaining about any setbacks instead of trusting God to use them for His glory and our good
- Living with an acute or chronic sense of anxiety because things aren't going as we planned

Of course, the list could go on for many pages. Most of us would look at the list and immediately say, "That's not me! I don't do that!" But at least take time to think and pray. Invite the Spirit to shine His light on the recesses of your heart. You may have hidden your actions and attitudes from people, but not from Him.

As you contemplate these flaws, it may help to consider how much the *opposite* traits are true (or not) in your life. For instance, gossip is spreading information, true or false, designed to tear down another person. The opposite is to keep your mouth shut or go to the person and speak the truth in love. Ruthless gratitude is the opposite of complaining. You get the picture.

To the extent we are broken before the Lord, to that extent and no more are we open to the flood of the Spirit's love, forgiveness, acceptance, and power to change. In most cases, a new culture in a church begins with a renewed heart in the pastor.

To the extent we are broken before the Lord, to that extent and no more are we open to the flood of the Spirit's love, forgiveness, acceptance, and power to change.

ROLLING OUT THE STRATEGY

I can imagine a pastor or church leader reading this far in the book and thinking, *I'm going to start all this today!* I applaud the enthusiasm, but I have a very strong recommendation: Don't! Before you think about implementing any strategy, find someone to help you internalize the principles of a Spirit-filled life—not just the power and holiness, but the weakness and vulnerability. You may think you've got it all covered, but a gifted mentor can take you deeper . . . sometimes much deeper. Where do you find this kind of mentor? An old Chinese proverb says, "When the student is ready, the teacher will appear." If you're ready, ask God to give you the person you need to mentor you. The right person will appear at the right time. It may not be your best friend or someone widely known and respected. The Lord may bring someone you never expected. Be open to His leading.

I don't think Scott would have picked me to be his mentor in the things of the Spirit. In some ways, we're like oil and water. But God led us to become friends, and both of us have benefited greatly from our relationship. Actually, I knew for over a year that God wanted me to step into Scott's life, but the time wasn't right. When the Spirit prompted both Scott and me, we were both ready. We began as mentor and student, but now we're partners.

Jesus told us to ask, seek, and knock. If we're hungry for God, He will send someone to feed us with the manna of the Spirit and quench our thirst with the overflow of living water.

You can't roll out the comprehensive strategy all at once. I believe God gives us benchmarks as signs we're ready to take the next steps. When each of these is met, we can move to the next one. If we try to do too much too soon, we'll probably confuse our people, erode trust, and set the plan back several months. This is the process you can expect:

1. First, you'll recognize a genuine hunger for God. Open your heart to the Lord and ask Him to reveal Himself to you. (You're probably already there, or you wouldn't have read this far in the book.)

2. Find a trusted mentor to prod you to be more honest than you've ever been before. The Lord will lead you to someone to help you expose the desires and sins of your heart, and you'll experience brokenness and healing. This isn't a "one shot" deal. The Lord is patient and persistent. If your heart remains open, He will peel back layers of self-deception as you continue to pray, seek, and talk to your mentor. Over time, become competent in two essential skills that are often overlooked: confession and repentance.

3. The first evidence of real, significant, persistent change is that your family will notice something different in your attitudes and actions. They will probably welcome the change, but it may also create turmoil. Even positive change is often hard for a spouse and kids to take. Give them time. They're looking for authenticity, faithfulness, tenderness, and consistency. Empty words aren't enough.

4. Your leaders will realize you're more interested in God's glory and experiencing His presence than in attendance, the success of programs, and the budget. The way you lead staff meetings, board meetings,

Your leaders will realize you're more interested in God's glory and experiencing His presence than in attendance, the success of programs, and the budget.

worship services, and every other event at the church will change because you're changing. Some leaders and volunteers will love it, but some may feel confused or threatened by your new values and passion.

5. As your leaders notice the change in you, share what God is doing in your life. Tell them about the impact of your mentor, and ask the leaders to join you in pursuing God with all your heart and utilizing the gifts of the Spirit. Begin to build a small team of people who share your heart for a new day of Spirit-led living. These people may be on your board (or maybe not!), your staff team, your top volunteers, or a group of trusted friends who are part of your ministry. Build a bridgehead for a new culture, and expand from there. Ask them to meet with you regularly in the coming weeks for informal times of prayer.

6. Gradually expand the circle. With the support and believing prayers of the ones who have joined you, invite more leaders and volunteers in your ministry to open their hearts to the Spirit. Be patient. Expect confusion and resistance. Let them ask every question they can imagine, and thank them for asking, even if their tone is a bit offensive. They'll need time to process what you're asking them to do, just as it has taken you time to assimilate what it means to create a new culture. This is often a pivotal time in the transition of a church.

7. Out of the informal prayer gatherings, form the Core. Invite people to come, explain the purpose and process, and start praying regularly with them. Find a time that works best for you and for them, and dive in. Ask them for a three-month commitment. At the end of this time, reevaluate, and ask them for a longer commitment.

8. At the end of three months, let each person in the Core invite a trusted friend to join the group. Take time in the first meeting to explain the principles and practices to the expanded group, and answer their questions. Some may not feel comfortable joining the prayer team. That's perfectly fine. Love them and affirm them. Don't let there be even a hint of "insiders" and "outsiders." They may want to join later.

9. Recruit, select, and train competent mentors (probably from your Core) and invite people to a Freedom Quest—after you've attended one, of course. The number of mentors determines the size of your Freedom Quest. Don't push it. And remember: one mentor for each participant: men with men, women with women. After the event, shepherd the pairs of mentors and participants through the twelve weeks of follow up.

10. After the twelve weeks of follow-up teaching, training, and discipleship, consider inviting some or all of the participants to attend a semester of the School of Ministry.

11. Now the strategy is fully engaged: the Core meets weekly, a Freedom Quest is held twice a year, and the School of Ministry has two semesters a year, spring and fall.

Through all of this, a new normal, a new culture takes shape in your church. There will be many detours and delays, some disagreements and misunderstandings, inevitable confusion and conflict. This isn't a machine we can tool to run smoothly. We're dealing with people who are trying to walk with the living God and an enemy who opposes a vital, passionate, living faith.

How long does this take? As long as it needs to take. There are no rigid timelines and no deadlines. Your mentor will help you know if you're pushing too hard or you're too timid. I would expect the rollout to take at least a year, but I wouldn't be surprised if it takes two. Throughout this time, keep pursuing God with all your heart. Keep meeting with your mentor and grow deep roots of faith. Practice the gifts, and see who God brings to join you in the adventure.

ONE EXAMPLE

Our church has been implementing and refining our strategy for almost two decades. We've had the benefit of time to learn from trial and error, but maybe other churches don't have to repeat all the errors it took for us to learn the lessons! When Scott felt led to start a Core, Freedom Quests, and a School of Ministry, he told his staff about the entire strategy. His children's pastor and student pastor felt overwhelmed. They came to him and said, "Okay, we can see that this is going to be a huge change for our church, but we can't do it all today. What are the three things that are your top priorities for us for the next six months?"

Scott thought about it, and he came up with three steps to begin changing the culture at The Oaks, starting with the young people:

1. Every young person will be encouraged to pray in the Spirit on all occasions. It should be normal for Spirit-filled Christians to pray in the Spirit anytime, anywhere—not out loud or in a weird way, but quietly and consistently like Ephesians 6:18 commands us to do.
2. Every young person will learn to live with a prophetic awareness. People should know how to hear and recognize the voice of God so they can walk in obedience to His promptings. God will speak, heal, and minister through everyone who has this kind of Spirit awareness.
3. Young people will realize that church is where they are equipped for ministry, but life is where ministry happens. Everybody gets a flame so they can burn brightly in their businesses, schools, sports teams, and families.

Of course, Scott began implementing these things in worship services, classes and groups, and with every level of leadership at The Oaks, but he believes it's important to start young. And it may happen that "the children will lead" their parents in spiritual renewal as they come home and share what they're learning.

And it may happen that "the children will lead" their parents in spiritual renewal as they come home and share what they're learning.

To infuse Spirit-filled power and love into the church, every meeting can begin with prayer—not stale, lifeless words, but praying in the Spirit, loudly and demonstratively, to invite the Spirit of God to come among us in tenderness and might. Every ministry team can incorporate this kind of prayer in their meetings. It's not superfluous. It's essential if we're going to touch the heart of God and get His wisdom for our ministries. It reminds us that we're living in an upside-down kingdom, and ultimately, it's His agenda, not ours.

WHATEVER IT TAKES

We can read a lot of books on church growth, worship styles, and constructing sermons. We can find a lot of examples of pastors and other spiritual leaders who are doing a lot of things really well, but there may not be many who are open to being broken by the Lord and willing to implement a new culture of the Spirit. Find godly, humble leaders in your area and hang out with them. If the leaders you find aren't near you, ask if you can drive or fly there for a few days to soak up what they can impart to you.

If you're hungry, God may bring someone into your life, or you may search high and low until you find that person who can help you flow with the Spirit. Either way, God will provide.

Form a network of pastors and other church leaders who hunger and thirst for God, who are open to the Spirit's work to glorify Christ and empower believers with all the gifts. Pray with and for one another, and see what God will do. Clear the stage in your leadership to make room for the Holy Spirit to do wonders in and through you. Allow time and space for the gifts to operate. It will be amazing.

THINK ABOUT IT . . .

1. Why is it crucial to recognize and embrace the upside-down kingdom? What happens to our leadership when we pursue success, pleasure, and approval instead of God's glory?

2. How will identifying the benchmarks of progress help you?

3. Who do you know who can encourage you, inspire you, challenge you, and equip you?

CHAPTER 14

WORTH THE PRICE

On the broad spectrum of leadership styles and the complexity of church situations, we can identify three very different ways to pastor a church. Some try to be in complete control of every person and situation, squeezing spontaneity and life out of every aspect of worship and ministry. Some go to the other extreme. They think planning and organizing quenches the Spirit, so they assume they can just "let things happen." Both of these methods make the pastor feel safe and comfortable, but for opposite reasons: one feels threatened by any substantive change (or even a slight variation), and the other wants to avoid responsibility for the work of planning and making hard choices.

But there's a third way: the biblical, God-given role of pastoring the flock God has entrusted to us. When we do the hard but necessary work of providing spiritual leadership, we pay a price, but it's well worth it. We realize we're partners with God in the greatest adventure the world has ever known—seeking and saving the lost, building vibrant disciples, and establishing His kingdom of kindness, justice, and righteousness on earth.

As we consider the price we must pay to pray, listen, plan, and lead, the question for all of us is this: Is it worth it?

Our answer is an unqualified "Yes!"

THE BEST INVESTMENT

As Scott and I have trusted God to equip us and guide us as pastors of our two churches, we've had to invest time, heart, and energy into our people, but it's an investment that has paid huge dividends. In a nutshell, we've seen what we all long to see—we've seen God show up! God has spoken to and through our people, unbelievers have come to faith, shattered relationships have been restored, people have reached out to care for those less fortunate, and a spirit of holy, awesome worship has surrounded our churches.

As we've told our stories, some people have sheepishly asked, "Well, hasn't it been, you know, weird?"

We've responded, "It has been amazing, powerful, soul-stirring, and supernatural as God has worked in love and power among us. Is that what you mean by *weird*?"

Experiencing the supernatural shouldn't be weird to us. It should be SOP—standard operating procedure. To train the Twelve, Jesus sent them out in pairs with these instructions:

> "As you go, proclaim this message: 'The kingdom of heaven has come near.' Heal the sick, raise the dead, cleanse those who have leprosy, drive out demons. Freely you have received; freely give." (Matt. 10:7–8)

Before Jesus ascended to the Father, He spoke to the disciples and told them,

> "Go into all the world and preach the gospel to all creation. Whoever believes and is baptized will be saved, but whoever does not believe will be condemned. And these signs will accompany those who believe: In my name they will drive out demons; they will speak in new tongues; they will pick up snakes with their hands; and when they drink deadly poison, it will not hurt them at all; they will place their hands on sick people, and they will get well." (Mark 16:15–18)

Matthew's account of the conversation just before the ascension added Jesus' directive to His command to make disciples of all nations: "and teaching them to obey everything I have commanded you" (Matt. 28:20). "Everything" surely includes the Great Commandment and the Great Commission, but His followers couldn't fulfill these commands without the power of the Holy Spirit. We may live twenty centuries later, but the command to teach "everything" still stands.

The supernatural life is "normal" for those who are filled with the Spirit, in love with Jesus Christ, and submissive to the Father's will. When we get a taste of this kind of power and love in our own lives, it will spill out into the lives of those around us. And when many others in our churches experience the Spirit's presence, love, and power, those things will overflow into their families, coworkers, and neighbors—they will see a tidal wave of transformed lives!

The supernatural life is "normal" for those who are filled with the Spirit, in love with Jesus Christ, and submissive to the Father's will.

These things, however, don't just happen. They require pastors and leaders to be humble before the Lord, earnestly seek His face, and ask Him to empower them with His Spirit. They have to pay a price, but they soon discover it's the best investment they could ever make.

The first leaders of the church knew they needed to be good pastors to their people. On the day of Pentecost, tongues of fire descended on the 120 disciples in the upper room, and they spoke the gospel to the Jewish pilgrims in their own languages. Peter stood up to preach the good news.

The people were confused by what they had seen and heard, so Peter began, "Let me explain this to you; listen carefully to what I say" (Acts 2:14). He didn't make any assumptions they would "get it" sooner or later. He stepped in and spoke up to teach truth and correct erroneous thinking.

At the end of Peter's powerful, prophetic gospel message, the Spirit convicted many hearts, and they asked, "Brothers, what shall we do?" (Acts 2:37) Again, Peter pastored the people by explaining the next step of faith: "Repent and be baptized, every one of you, in the name of Jesus Christ for the forgiveness of your sins. And you will receive the gift of the Holy Spirit. The promise is for you and your children and for all who are far off—for all whom the Lord our God will call" (Acts 2:38–39).

We can see the work of the Spirit in Peter's life even on this first day of being Spirit-filled and Spirit-led. Instead of being impulsive and reactionary, he continued to patiently and persistently speak to the needs of his new flock. Luke tells us, "With many other words he warned them; and he pleaded with them, 'Save yourselves from this corrupt generation.' Those who accepted his message were baptized, and about three thousand were added to their number that day" (Acts 2:40–41).

Of course, Paul's first letter to the Corinthians contains clear, extended teaching about how to use the gifts. In chapter 12, he lists the gifts and provides instructions about them; in chapter 13, he warns the Corinthians to avoid expressing the gifts apart from genuine love; and in chapter 14, he provides detailed directives about how to use the gifts, especially in public. From Paul's point of view, the point of the gifts isn't to be sensational, but to build up the church in every way.

COMMON FEARS

Many pastors have backed away from teaching on speaking in tongues and prophecy because they're afraid people will do bizarre things in their church, and consequently, embarrass them and God. If we open our hearts and our church life to express the gifts, unusual things can and probably will happen—but that doesn't mean we should throw the baby out with the bathwater. Putting a clamp on the work of the Spirit robs us of countless opportunities to let Him do marvelous things among us. The goal, then, isn't to eliminate weirdness, but to limit it, manage it, and help people learn valuable lessons when it happens.

The goal, then, isn't to eliminate weirdness, but to limit it, manage it, and help people learn valuable lessons when it happens.

In one of Scott's services, a man brought a shofar into the auditorium. In the middle of the sermon, the man gave several long, earsplitting blasts! The interruption was his attempt to offer praise to the Lord, but instead of bringing encouragement to the congregation, it freaked them out. Scott had to pastor the situation privately and ask the man to stop playing the shofar during the service because it was distracting people from worship.

In my teen years I heard a woman, attempting to give an interpretation of tongues, arrogantly yell, "The Lord says, 'I'll have the last laugh!'" Similarly, a person in our church gave a prophetic word, but the tone was anything but encouraging, strengthening, and comforting. His words said, "God loves you," but his voice and the look on his face were very harsh. This blend of anger and compassion are a confusing and destructive message. That's not the voice of the Lord. I went to the man after the service to help him understand that he didn't have to sound harsh to be used prophetically. I asked him, "Do you think God is mad at us?"

He thought for a second and then responded, "I don't think so."

I explained, "You sounded angry when you spoke, even though God was saying He loved us."

Many people were exposed to harsh prophetic pronouncements when they were growing up, so they assume that's the way God speaks all the time. They need clear teaching and patient pastoring so they will know better.

In some traditional Pentecostal churches, "dancing in the Spirit" was expressed with reckless abandon—in fact, the more reckless the better. People ran around, moved their bodies frenetically, ran into walls, jumped over pews, the whole bit. In my dad's church, Sunday nights were the most common time for such behavior. During one of the services, a large lady got up with her baby in her arms and began dancing wildly. Suddenly she tripped and fell on the baby. In seconds, the baby stopped breathing and began turning blue. The lady screamed incessantly. My dad stepped in and said, "Give me the baby, and take her to a back room."

As some people escorted the mother out of the room, my dad turned to the congregation and said, "Tomorrow morning we *will not* read in the paper about a church killing a baby in a Sunday night service. We'll ask God to bring this baby back to life." I was only ten years old, so all this was fascinating to me. Dad was very calm. He prayed for about a minute, and then the baby began crying and color returned to its face. It had been a miracle of necessity, not choice.

The Scriptures teach and describe instances of dancing in the Spirit as a wonderful expression of worship—but it isn't "in the Spirit" when it becomes distracting, sensual, or out of control. Everything is to be done decently and in order (1 Cor. 14:40).

I could list and describe other bizarre behaviors that have happened throughout my thirty-five years of ministry, but none of them come close to the unusual activity Paul had to confront in the Corinthian church. According to what we read in his first letter to them, Paul said they were giving God a bad name in the way they handled the gifts in their services. However, that didn't mean Paul wanted them to stop the flow of the Spirit altogether. In fact, he encouraged them, "Therefore, my brothers and sisters, be eager to prophesy, and do not forbid speaking in tongues. But everything should be done in a fitting and orderly way" (1 Cor. 14:39–40).

PASTOR THE GIFTS

The fear of weirdness was exactly the reason Scott called me the week after he announced "a new day" at The Oaks. He had seen enough strange things in his experience as a pastor's son and as a pastor, and he wasn't willing to allow odd, offensive behavior to ruin the good things God was doing in his church. He was open to a new way of letting the Spirit work in grace and power, but he needed guidelines—for himself, his leaders, and all the people who attend The Oaks.

We developed the Rules of Engagement to help pastors, first Scott and me, conduct our services decently and with order. Pastors have every reason to be concerned about bizarre behavior happening when people are learning to use the gifts in public settings. These Rules help us train our leaders, guide our people, limit weirdness, and lovingly correct people who try to color outside the lines. They give structure so the gifts can build up instead of pushing people away.

We want people to be amazed at the grace, love, wisdom, and power of God. We want the expression of the gifts to cause "the secrets of their hearts [to be] laid bare. So they will fall down and worship God, exclaiming, 'God is really among you (1 Cor. 14:25)!'" We don't want them to come to our services and say, "You are out of your mind" (1 Cor. 14:23).

Some pastors react to these guidelines and insist, "That's quenching the Spirit!" I don't agree. Leading, shepherding, and training people to use the gifts only quench expressions *driven by the flesh*. The guidelines actually unleash the Spirit.

Here's the point: pastors and other church leaders can't assume they can just leave their people to have spontaneous, free expressions of the gifts. They are pastors, and part of their God-given role is to lead their people in the use of the gifts. The gifts are like gasoline, sources of power that can be effectively used to move people in a positive direction or used ineffectively to destroy. Pastors must establish order, otherwise, according to the law of entropy, disorder is inevitable.

The gifts are like gasoline, sources of power that can be effectively used to move people in a positive direction or used ineffectively to destroy.

When something is out of order, it's not the end of the world. It's an opportunity to shepherd the people who need teaching and direction. A lady in Scott's church began speaking in tongues during the altar call. She was weeping as she spoke loudly for a minute, then two minutes, and then three minutes. Scott went over to her and patted her on the shoulder. He said, "Thank you for sharing your gift. Now we need to wait for the interpretation."

The interpretation from someone in the room was short and direct: "The Lord says, 'I will set you free.'"

After the service, Scott talked to her. She wasn't upset Scott had stopped her. Actually, she was excited! She told him, "I'm from a religious background that has no experience with the gifts. I gave my heart to the Lord a few months ago, and I was baptized in the Holy Spirit at a Wednesday night prayer meeting. I don't know how to use the gifts. This morning, I was just doing the best I know how."

Scott responded, "That's fantastic! Let me explain something that might help you. You did great on your timing of expressing the gift because I asked if anyone had something from the Lord. But it seemed that you were having a private prayer moment with the Lord . . . in front of everyone. I think that's what you were doing, wasn't it?"

She said, "Yes, it sure was. I'm so sorry."

Scott assured her, "That's perfectly fine. This is the way we learn. There was no harm done at all. You were crying out to the Lord, and He promised to set you free. That's so cool!"

She paused for a second and then smiled, "Thank you for helping me learn how to use my gift!"

All of the elements of the strategy—the Core, Freedom Quest, the twelve weeks of teaching and discipleship, and the School of Ministry—teach and equip people to use their gifts in every arena: privately, in church, and in the marketplace. These meetings, events, mentoring, and groups provide a safe place, a kind of "gifts lab," for people to experiment, try, fail, and learn. The Rules of Engagement give clear direction to everyone about how the gifts should be expressed in the public setting.

Pastors, it's your role to lead your church in the expression of the gifts. It's your role to model and train people, and it's your role to lead in public worship. For instance, when you sense God wants to speak prophetically in a worship service, stop and tell the people, "We're going to be quiet now. I sense God wants to say something to us. Three things might happen: there may be a prophetic word, there may be a gift of tongues and an interpretation, or we may simply remain quiet for a while and let the Lord speak to each of us individually."

If someone gives a word of prophecy, the pastor can repeat it, confirm it, and invite people to respond to the word in faith. If part of the word seems to be off target, the pastor should repeat and confirm only the part that was from God. It's not the right time to correct the person or comment on the part that may have been from the flesh.

If God gives a tongue and an interpretation, it's a divine altar call for the unbelievers in the room. The pastor can explain to the congregation, "According to 1 Corinthians 14:22, what you just heard is a sign to those who don't yet know the Lord." To address their possible fears and confusion, the pastor might ask, "For how many of you was this the first time you've ever heard something like this?" A few people may raise their hands.

Then the pastor can ask, "How many of you have come today to check out the Christian faith and see if it's something you want to pursue?" And most of the same people raise their hands.

The pastor can then explain, "The Bible says that what you just heard is a sign from God for the people who just raised their hands, the unfamiliar and the not yet believing. Let me again emphasize the interpretation." The pastor can repeat the exact words or explain the gospel using common terminology.

The pastor doesn't want to miss this holy moment: "If you sense God has just spoken to you, I want to meet you at the altar right now. It doesn't matter whether this is the 'right time' in the service. God just showed you He loves you so much that He's changing our service just for you." The pastor invites people to come forward and prays over them as they give their hearts to Christ.

WHAT DO YOU DO WHEN . . . ?

Even with the best of planning and preparation, on rare occasions, weirdness happens. Let me describe some events and offer some suggestions.

A person gives a prophetic word in a harsh tone.

This mixed message confuses people, especially those who are new to the faith and the gifts. If the message is good and right, confirm it, but assure people that God's message is one of hope, love, and kindness. Talk to the person privately after the service and ask what's going on in his or her life. Quite often, internalized stress and anger has spilled out in an inappropriate way and time. A loving conversation with some gentle probing questions may uncover long-buried wounds and fears that can now be addressed with truth and grace.

If you sense God has actually given someone a prophetic word of judgment, it should always be delivered with tears of sorrow and a gracious invitation to repent, not harsh condemnation.

A person speaks in King James English.

Some people still believe the apostle Paul carried a King James Bible. They love the cadence and wording, but they're not sensitive to the people around them who live in the modern world. Their hearts are usually right, but they lack perception about how they come across. A pastor can go to these people after the service to affirm their heart and message. Then the pastor can say, "Thank you so much for sharing with our people. I think they will be able to hear the word better if you speak in a conversational way. I know you love the old Bible, but most people today use modern translations. The next time God gives you a word, would you try to give it in a conversational way? I would appreciate it, and the people listening will receive it much better."

Someone prophesies or speaks in tongues too long.

Like Scott did with the woman who spoke too long in his church, you can walk over and gently stop the person. If it's a word of prophecy, summarize the message and invite the audience to respond. If it's a tongue, ask for an interpretation. After the service, find this person and affirm, "Thank you for participating in worship by expressing the gift. That's fantastic!" Then you can explain, "Let me help you understand how the Lord wants to use you even more effectively."

The vast majority of people are happy to be affirmed and instructed, and they appreciate a pastor's kind instructions.

The vast majority of people are happy to be affirmed and instructed, and they appreciate a pastor's kind instructions.

A gift of tongues isn't immediately followed by an interpretation.

An expression of tongues given in a public setting should always have an interpretation. After a person has spoken in tongues, you can say simply, "And now we wait for the interpretation." If one doesn't come, explain, "The interpretation is out there among us, and we'll wait for it." If you sense the person has simply been speaking a private prayer language in public, you can say, "I believe this tongue is a wonderful expression of praise. Let's join our brother (or sister) in praising God." You can then offer a prayer of thanksgiving or lead a song. After the service, meet with the person to affirm his or her heart of praise and explain the use of the gift of tongues in public. A private prayer language is for private expressions of praise and petition.

If, however, you sense the tongue was genuine, but even after a time of waiting no interpretation is given, take a minute to explain that it's important for people to be obedient and speak up if God has given them an interpretation. They may feel uncomfortable speaking in public, but God will use them in a powerful way if they will obey. In this case, don't communicate frustration about a person's disobedience. Instead, offer gracious instruction and assurance. Maybe the person will respond next time. Also, privately encourage the person giving the message in tongues to pray for the interpretation (1 Cor. 14:13).

More than three people utter corporate-wide tongues in church.

After the third person gives an utterance in tongues in a worship service and there has been an interpretation each time, occasionally another person begins to speak. In this case, it is our responsibility to be proactive, mentioning Paul's instruction to have no more than three (1 Cor. 14:27). We may say, "I sense the Lord still wants to say something to us. Since we've had three tongues and interpretations, maybe the Lord wants to give us a prophetic word." And we wait to see if God does, indeed, have a word for us.

Noted Pentecostal scholar Dr. Anthony Palma underscores Paul's instructions to us: "These charismatic manifestations are not to be so numerous as to usurp the place of the normal exposition and reading of Scriptures .... The limitation ... is to keep these gifts from dominating a service in which other elements of worship ought also to be observed."[16]

A prophetic word isn't mixed with spirit and flesh; it's pure evil.

When Scott was a boy, a man got up in his church, pointed to his dad, the pastor, and announced through clenched teeth, "That man is not of God! Don't listen to him! And these people (pointing to the elders) are demonic!" On those exceptionally rare occasions, public rebuke and correction are absolutely necessary.

Scott's dad told the man, "Your words are not from the Lord. You need to sit down and be quiet." His father then turned to the congregation and explained, "I'm not sure what that's about, but I assure you that his message isn't from God. You can judge for yourselves. God's message is full of faith, hope, and love. Right now, we're going to sing a song and pray in the Spirit. And ask God to work His grace deep into this man's heart."

A person is defiant.

When Scott began the "new day" at The Oaks and shared the Rules of Engagement with the church, a lady who attended the early morning traditional service privately told a friend, "I'm not going to let Pastor Scott quench the Spirit in me! I'm going to use my gift any way I feel led!"

The next week she attended the first service on Sunday morning. Scott had explained to the church that God never interrupts Himself, so He won't lead anyone to speak while He is speaking. But this lady was determined to do her thing. She got up in the middle of Scott's sermon and began speaking in tongues loudly—and she kept going and going. Scott stopped speaking. He walked over and sat next to her for a very long time until she finally finished. He then stood up and said, "And now we'll wait for the interpretation." It didn't come. They waited . . . and waited even more. After five long minutes, the woman was noticeably getting nervous. Finally, a man stood up and said, "The Lord is saying, 'Why are you going against the new thing I want to do in this church? Will you continue to be in rebellion?'"

Scott said, "I'm sure all of you know that this message wasn't an interpretation. This is a prophetic word. God is calling us to submit to the new thing He is doing. Let's all open our hearts to His leading." Then he asked everyone in the room to check their hearts and surrender everything to the Lord. We can't be stubborn and defiant when it comes to following Christ.

The woman wrote Scott a note the next week and told him she had found a church that let her use her gifts however she wanted to use them. The others sitting in the service that morning were glad they had a leader who would lovingly handle situations that could potentially create distraction and disruption.

Only on very rare occasions should correction be public. When someone speaks evil or there is the presence of a demonic influence, the pastor immediately needs to address those issues. In all other situations, we publicly affirm what is good and then privately repeat our affirmation and provide instruction about the proper expression of the gifts. The tone of the pastor usually determines the response of the person. If we're gentle and kind, the response is often humble submission and gratitude. If we're harsh and impatient, the person usually responds with defensiveness or is crushed by our words (or both).

WORTH IT?

Some pastors don't want to take the time and trouble to engage people with affirmation, teaching, and correction. They already feel stressed out by all the demands of the role, and adding a shepherding role regarding spiritual gifts seems like too much to handle. Instead, they abdicate their God-given responsibility, refusing to permit the use of gifts or letting things get out of hand. Neither of these approaches serves God's purposes.

If pastors don't oversee this part of the ministry, the lady who prays in tongues too long will do it the next week and the next, and the man who gives harsh pronouncements will continue in a spirit of judgment. Eventually, exasperated board members will ask the pastor, "Why are you letting these people ruin our church?" Under pressure, he shuts it all down. Stopping it all is easier, he's sure, than shepherding, teaching, training, and lovingly correcting people.

Teaching people to express the gifts is part of our God-given privilege and responsibility as His under-shepherds, and frankly, it's one of the most fulfilling, thrilling parts of the role.

Failing to give proper instruction is not the answer. Teaching people to express the gifts is part of our God-given privilege and responsibility as His under-shepherds, and frankly, it's one of the most fulfilling, thrilling parts of the role.

Leaders, pastor this dimension! Don't neglect the gifts, and don't be afraid of what will happen when you invite your people to exercise them. Don't just throw the door open and see what happens. Take your people through the laboratory of teaching, training, modeling, and experimentation to show them how to express the gifts. Then, when they do, continue to shepherd them with grace and truth.

There's a learning curve in all this, just as there has been a learning curve for every other aspect of ministry. Read, learn, talk to friends, find a mentor, take steps of faith, make corrections, and learn more each step of the way.

God has marvelous things to say *to* and *through* your people as you lead them to exercise the gifts. Don't miss what the Spirit wants to do in your church.

THINK ABOUT IT . . .

1. How would you identify and describe the benefits of leading the people in your church to flow in the gifts?

2. How do the Rules of Engagement give you confidence to lead your people in expressing the gifts?

3. What are your hopes and fears as you think about the potential—and the price—of people in your church using the gifts? How would you define your role in shepherding your people in this area?

SECTION 5

NOW WHAT?

(BOTH VOICES)

CHAPTER 15

WHO WILL YOU SERVE?

JOHN . . .

Joshua was one of the greatest leaders the world has ever known. Most people who follow gifted leaders never come out of the long shadows of their predecessors. No one remembers who followed coach Bear Bryant at Alabama or Woody Hayes at Ohio State. Probably no one thought Moses' successor would be remembered, either, but Joshua proved to be a brilliant commander and a gifted administrator.

We wouldn't expect people wandering in the desert their whole lives to be brave and effective soldiers, but Joshua led them in the conquest of the Promised Land. He distributed the land and marked the boundaries, but his role wasn't finished. He renewed the covenant God made with Abraham, Isaac, and Jacob, and he gave a charge to all the people. He told them,

> "Now fear the LORD and serve him with all faithfulness. Throw away the gods your ancestors worshiped

> beyond the Euphrates River and in Egypt, and serve the Lord. But if serving the Lord seems undesirable to you, then choose for yourselves this day whom you will serve, whether the gods your ancestors served beyond the Euphrates, or the gods of the Amorites, in whose land you are living. But as for me and my household, we will serve the Lord." (Josh. 24:14–15)

Centuries later, Paul had the same concern for God's people. He knew they could easily be deceived by the lure of success, pleasure, and approval . . . or anything else that looks more attractive than the grace of God. In very personal and passionate terms, he wrote the Christians in Corinth:

> I am jealous for you with a godly jealousy. I promised you to one husband, to Christ, so that I might present you as a pure virgin to him. But I am afraid that just as Eve was deceived by the serpent's cunning, your minds may somehow be led astray from your sincere and pure devotion to Christ. (2 Cor. 11:2–3)

As pastors and leaders, we might think this admonition is only for us to speak to the people in our churches, but it's just as much for us. We can serve other gods, and our hearts can be fixed on desires leading us away from God. The size of the church, the applause of people, or a good reputation in the denomination can all begin to mean more to us than

God's love and approval. Our role as pastors isn't about gifts or power or strategies; it's about choosing God as our ultimate delight.

If Joshua or Paul were in the room with us today, I believe they would look us in the eye and ask us hard questions about what's really in our hearts. It's easy to say we serve God. After all, we're in the ministry, and we work hard on all the services and programs. But the externals don't necessarily show the internals. It's easy to drift, to slide from passion to complacency, from ardent love to just getting the job done, from delighting in God to fearing disapproval of people. When this happens, we lose our cutting edge. Wonder—laughing, weeping, glad wonder at the astonishing grace of God is essential. In his book, *Dangerous Wonder,* Mike Yaconelli commented, "The greatest enemy of Christianity may be people who say they believe in Jesus but who are no longer astonished and amazed."[17]

If you choose to go hard after God, you'll experience more adversity than you would encounter if you played it safe, but you'll delight in more power and love than you ever dreamed possible.

If you choose to go hard after God, you'll experience more adversity than you would encounter if you played it safe, but you'll delight in more power and love than you ever dreamed possible. You won't be disappointed, and you'll never be the same. When we operate in the gifts of the Spirit—when we clear the stage in our leadership and turn the page to a new day in our lives and ministries—we no longer see the world in monochromatic black and white; we see in vivid, living color. The old way of doing life and ministry no longer works. We know too much to go back. We've tasted something far sweeter, and nothing less will satisfy. Our consuming passion has become the glory of God, the honor of God, the smile of God, the face of God. Nothing else will do.

Paradoxically, we'll become more aware of sin in our lives because we'll be more in tune with the Spirit. We'll be able to be more honest because we'll know we are secure in God's love. Temptation will always be there, but we'll realize we have more authority over our thoughts, our desires, and the Enemy's schemes. When we sin, we'll be quicker to confess it, genuinely sorry we have hurt God's heart, and we'll repent with gladness instead of shame.

SCOTT . . .

Several weeks after God gave me the message to "clear the stage" and to announce "a new day" for our church, John came to speak at The Oaks to challenge our people—and especially my family and me—to serve Him only. It was a powerful message from the book of Joshua. He brought

Jenni, Dillon, Hunter, Dakota, and me on the stage to ask each of us if we were willing to serve God supremely. I really appreciated the way he handled this. He didn't use an ounce of guilt or manipulation. In fact, he turned to our people and said, "Is it okay with you if one or more of Scott's family says, 'No, I don't want to serve the Lord'? Will you still love them and encourage them?" The people cheered and shouted, "Yes!" We felt so loved.

John asked each of us about our commitment to put Jesus first. Then he turned to Dillon and asked him to share what God was doing in his life. In this totally unrehearsed moment, Dillon took the microphone and said,

> I went to college three years ago. I was nine hours away from home. My parents weren't there, so I had a choice to do whatever I wanted—and no one would ever know. No one knew I was a pastor's kid unless I told them. It gave me the freedom to live the life I really wasn't able to live here because everyone knew I was Pastor Scott Wilson's son.
>
> I made some bad choices, and I made some mistakes—some that I'm not proud of at all, and I would be very embarrassed for you to know about them. But God used them to make me into the person I am today. I believe I went away from home for a reason. I needed to find God for myself, and I needed to figure out who I was and what I was going to be—and

not just live in the shadow of my dad and my mom. Three years of living the life that people dream of living, one many would say is a perfect life, was really empty and worthless. You just keep going for more and more, but you're never truly satisfied.

Yesterday I had breakfast with Pastor John. He said, "Dillon, it's time to draw a line in the sand. It's time for you to decide if you're going to cross that line and live for God, or if you're going to stay behind and live a mediocre life."

I've being thinking and praying about Pastor John's challenge for the last twenty-four hours.

This morning, I'm here to declare to you that I'm going to live for the Lord—and my future family, whenever that happens, is going to live for the Lord.

I know you guys don't have twenty-four hours to think and pray about it like I did. But in these next few moments, it's time for you to draw the line in the sand; it's time to get real with God. There are a lot of families in here. I don't think this choice is only for individuals. It's a family matter. It's a big choice, and like Pastor John said, there's no turning back when you decide to make it.

I didn't plan to speak this morning, but the weight that's lifted off my shoulders is giving me the freedom and the ability to speak truth right now, and it's the best feeling I've had in my life. There's nothing better

> than being real. So right now, I feel like the Lord is telling us that as families, we can come together and declare who we will serve.
>
> There may be a couple of people in your family who aren't on the same page about following Christ, but each person can respond to the invitation to put God first. There's nothing more powerful than this. As a family, decide right now whom you will serve. I'm telling you that you'll feel real—and you'll feel God's grace on your life.

As Dillon spoke, I dropped to my knees and wept tears of joy. People in the church were almost as touched as I was. They were yelling and cheering and shouting praise to the Lord. I was so happy. I think Dillon thought I was losing it. He came over to me and said, "Dad, it's going to be all right."

I looked at him and said, "I know, son. It already is."

John's son Nehemiah was our worship leader that morning. During all of this, he was singing Bonnie Raitt's song, "I Can't Make You Love Me." It was exactly the message John was preaching. God can't make us love Him. He graciously invites us to come to Him and respond to His love, but He lets each of us walk away if we choose. Dillon—and hundreds of others that morning—chose to love God, walk with Him, and serve Him with all their might.

Let's back up and look at the events that occurred before that amazing Sunday morning. Long before this powerful service, God had lovingly been leading the elders of The Oaks and me through a supernatural process of surrender and submission. I don't think this breakthrough service could have happened if we hadn't been obedient to what God was telling us to do. Weeks before, a man from John's church named Jason had a vision while he was passing by our church on his way to work. In the vision, I was standing on the roof of the church with my hands up to the air in a posture that said, "I'm in charge here!" Then I lowered my hands to my sides with a posture that said, "I can't do this." The Lord spoke to Jason and said, "I have warring angels I will send to watch over the people of The Oaks if Scott will get down and let Me do it."

Jason told John about the vision and the word of the Lord for me. John contacted me and asked if I wanted to go up on the roof of the church to reenact the vision. I said, "Absolutely."

We met at the church and climbed up the ladder to get to the roof. I lifted my hands up and then down to my side. I prayed, "Lord, I can't lead this place and take Your people where You want them to go. You have to lead us." After I prayed, I looked over at Red Oak High School, then my eyes swept over to the City Hall in Red Oak, and then to the new hospital going up in Waxahachie, several miles away. I had never been on our roof before, and I'd never had such a view.

John asked me, "What are you feeling as you look at all this?"

I answered, "I feel helpless." I prayed, "God, I can't handle all the drugs, alcohol, family issues, political issues, and health issues going on in this county. We need You!" Then I told the Lord, "I invite the warring angels to come and take their rightful place. I willingly step down and take my rightful place as the Lead Follower of The Oaks."

The next day, Jason called John with a report: "I drove by The Oaks today, and God showed me a vision of Pastor Scott climbing down the ladder on the side of the building. Just giving you the latest update."

Two weeks later, I was in my office in a prayer time getting ready for a morning meeting, and God told me to lie down on the floor like a dead man. I knew this act of obedience was a symbol of dying to myself. I got on the floor, and I prayed, "Lord, I die to myself and all that I want. The Oaks is Yours, Lord. And I'm Yours."

The next day, Jason had another vision while driving by the church. He called John and said, "I'm not sure what this means, but Pastor Scott is lying down on the ground beside the church. He's facing up like he's dead. I think that's good, but I'm not sure. Anyway, that's what I saw."

A few weeks later, Jason had a dream while he was sleeping. He saw me lying on the platform inside the church, and all of the Worship Center walls disappeared. Only the foundation was left. In his dream, all the people in the church saw me lying on the ground with no building around me. They followed my lead. As they all lay down on their backs, thousands of angels surrounded the Worship Center where the building's walls had been. The angels were standing all around us.

The next Sunday morning while John and I were praying in my office before the 8:30 a.m. service, another man in his church texted him: "I just saw a vision of thousands of angels all around the sanctuary at The Oaks."

During the day, a lady in our church wrote me a note to tell me she had a vision of countless angels in the worship service. When the service ended, the angels went home with the people. They're with us everywhere!

What a confirmation of what God was doing in me and in our church!

I don't believe this message of God's presence and power—and our humility and submission—is unique to me. It applies to all of us. God is calling you to spiritually get down off the roof of your church and your home and lay your life and family down before Him. He will come and hover over your house, angels will make up the walls of your life, and the Lord will do miraculous things in you—if you will completely and humbly submit your life to Him.

Leader, you have a decision. Who are you going to serve? Make sure you serve the only One worthy of your love and loyalty. Are you going to build Christ's church based on your own wisdom and your best efforts, or will you invite the Spirit of God to work in power in you and through you? Are you willing to clear the stage of all your props? God doesn't need your advice and help to do what He wants to do. But in His grace, He invites you to be His partner—a junior partner, but still a partner—if you're willing to say only what God tells you to say and do only what God tells you to do. It's time to get on the ground, to die to self, and ask God to do what only He can do. This is the way the Great Commandment and the Great Commission are fulfilled.

Are you going to build Christ's church based on your own wisdom and your best efforts, or will you invite the Spirit of God to work in power in you and through you?

Our prayer for you is the one Paul prayed for the believers in Ephesus. Let this be our benediction, our hope, and our challenge:

> That's why, when I heard of the solid trust you have in the Master Jesus and your outpouring of love to all the followers of Jesus, I couldn't stop thanking God for you—every time I prayed, I'd think of you and give thanks. But I do more than thank. I ask—ask the

God of our Master, Jesus Christ, the God of glory—to make you intelligent and discerning in knowing him personally, your eyes focused and clear, so that you can see exactly what it is he is calling you to do, grasp the immensity of this glorious way of life he has for his followers, oh, the utter extravagance of his work in us who trust him—endless energy, boundless strength! (Eph. 1:15–19, *The Message*)

THINK ABOUT IT . . .

1. What are some "counterfeit gods" that look so appealing to people in our culture? What are some that look especially appealing to pastors and other spiritual leaders?

2. If you had been listening to Joshua or reading Paul's letter to the Corinthians, how would you have responded to the challenge to know, love, and serve God supremely? How are you responding today?

3. What is the next step for you as you think, pray, and apply the principles of this book?

ENDNOTES

1 Donald Gee, *Toward Pentecostal Unity* (Springfield, MO: Gospel Publishing House, 1961), 18.

2 Tim Keller, "Practical Grace" sermon series, www.gospelinlife.com/

3 J. I. Packer, *Knowing God* (Downers Grove, Illinois: InterVarsity Press, 1973), 196.

4 M. Paul Brooks, *Pentecostal Gifts & Ministries in a Postmodern Era* (Springfield, MO: Gospel Publishing House, 2003), 89.

5 "And Can It Be That I Should Gain," Charles Wesley, 1738.

6 You can download this information at http://theoaksonline.org/wp-content/uploads/2014/03/Spiritual-Gifts-Service-Etiquette.pdf.

7 C. S. Lewis, *Voyage of the Dawn Treader* (New York: Harper Collins, 1952), 115–116.

8 Jack Hayford, *Worship His Majesty* (Ventura, CA: Regal, 2000), 60.

9 Christopher J. H. Wright, *Knowing the Holy Spirit Through the Old Testament* (Downers Grove, IL: InterVarsity Press, 2006), 63.

10 Watchman Nee, *Spiritual Authority,* (N. Chesterfield, VA: Christian Fellowship Publishers, Inc., 1972), 86.

11 Ibid., 50.

12 Charles Wesley, "O for a Thousand Tongues to Sing," 1739.

13 Wright, op. cit., 116–117.

14 Brooks, op. cit., 92.

15 Jack Deere, *Surprised by the Voice of God* (Grand Rapids: Zondervan, 1998), 239.

16 Anthony D. Palma, *The Holy Spirit: A Pentecostal Perspective* (Springfield, MO: Gospel Publishing House, 2001), 247

17 Mike Yaconelli, *Dangerous Wonder* (Colorado Springs: Navpress, 1998), 24–25.

ACKNOWLEDGEMENTS

A number of people have inspired us and helped to shape the concepts in this book, and we are very grateful. We want to thank . . .

Dr. George Wood and Dr. Jim Bradford for your input and encouragement on this project. We love and respect you so much.

Sol and Wini Arledge and Steve and Susan Blount for asking us to write the book and guiding us every step of the way.

Chris Railey, Heath Adamson, and Justin Lathrop for being our sounding board and wise advisors.

Dr. Paul Brooks for the hours you put into this book. We appreciate your expertise and wisdom. We are also grateful for the hours of prayers and your constant support as we lived out of this book in real time. You are an inspiration.

Pat Springle for being our friend and helping us shape the content. You are a phenomenal gift to the church and to both of us. We experienced amazing synergy the moment you got in the room with us, and you worked with us to craft every word. Without you it might not have ever seen the light of day. We are forever grateful.

The wonderful, loving, and faithful staff members and elders of our churches, The Oaks Fellowship and Freedom

Fellowship International. We are so grateful for your love, prayers, and support.

And most importantly we would like to thank God for giving us dear friends who sharpen us and never give up on us.

ABOUT THE AUTHORS

SCOTT WILSON

Scott Wilson has been in fulltime pastoral ministry for more than twenty-five years. He is the senior pastor of The Oaks Fellowship located in Dallas, Texas—now ministering to nearly 3,000 people each week.

Scott is the author of several books, including. *Ready, Set, Grow*; *Act Normal*; *The Next Level*; and *Steering Through Chaos*.

Scott and his wife, Jenni, have three boys: Dillon, Hunter, and Dakota. The Wilsons live in the Dallas area.

JOHN BATES

John Bates has been in full-time ministry since 1986. He accepted his second Lead Pastor position in 2003 at Freedom Fellowship International in Waxahachie, Texas. The church is prophetic in nature, abundant in resources, free in worship, large in purpose and submitted to the leadership of the Holy Spirit.

There is a deep love for taking the truth to the nations at FFI. As a result, John has ministered through crusades and pastoral leadership seminars in Central and Latin America, the Caribbean, Africa, Asia, and extensively throughout Europe.

Due to his focus on discipleship, John created Freedom Quest, consisting of a two-day Carpe Diem (seize the day) encounter with God. This event is followed by an intensive twelve-week mentorship. The results are men and women learning to experience freedom in Christ and learning how to walk said freedom out successfully.

Under John's leadership, FFI is now known as a praying church and sends teams throughout the world to conduct and lead prophetic prayer events. Prayer is the directing factor in John's life and ministry.

John and his wife, Shelli, live in the Dallas area where they parent Nehemiah, Eden, and their dog Cookie.

FOR MORE INFORMATION

For more information about these and other helpful resources, visit www.influenceresources.com

Ready, Set, Grow: Over a three-year-period, Wilson walked with his staff through a three-stage development process: modeling (year 1), mentoring (year 2), and multiplying (year 3). First, he writes, leaders must develop their own leadership capacities and become someone worth following. Then, they must lead their direct reports (whether staff or volunteer) through a similar developmental process. Finally, they need to create an environment where their direct reports are developing the people in their domain of ministry. A healthy church doesn't have to be a huge church, but it does need to be a growing church. *Ready, Set, Grow* will help you understand how to lead your church/ministry through a process of personal and organizational growth.

Act Normal: A thirty-one-day journey through the book of Acts, each day's reading discusses what it means to live for God and be empowered by the Holy Spirit. By expressing complex concepts in everyday language and using real-life examples, Scott Wilson helps you grasp the story that runs through Acts and teaches you how to live in a way that honors God

The Next Level: Learn to see the tests of life from God's perspective. Your times of pain and confusion aren't meant to be prisons that keep you from enjoying life. Instead, God wants to use them as classrooms to teach you the most valuable lessons you can ever learn.